IMAGES
of America

THE JEWISH COMMUNITY OF METRO DETROIT
1945–2005

IMAGES
of America

THE JEWISH COMMUNITY OF METRO DETROIT
1945–2005

Barry Stiefel

ARCADIA
PUBLISHING

Copyright © 2006 by Barry Stiefel
ISBN 978-1-5316-2432-3

Published by Arcadia Publishing
Charleston, South Carolina

Library of Congress Catalog Card Number: 2006920837

For all general information contact Arcadia Publishing at:
Telephone 843-853-2070
Fax 843-853-0044
E-mail sales@arcadiapublishing.com
For customer service and orders:
Toll-Free 1-888-313-2665

Visit us on the Internet at www.arcadiapublishing.com

Many authors dedicate their books to one's mother or wife—so I shall do both. I dedicate this book to my mother, Karen Stiefel, of blessed memory (1949–1995), who lived in the Metro Detroit area for most of her life; and to my beautiful bride, Lori Hoch Stiefel, who has been my pillar of support

CONTENTS

ACKNOWLEDGMENTS

I could not have done this book without the help of some very wonderful institutions and people in the Metro Detroit area. I thank the Leo M. Franklin Archives at Temple Beth El, Leonard N. Simons Jewish Community Archives at the Detroit Federation, Shaarey Zedek Archives, Sloan Museum and Archives of Flint, Michigan Region of B'nai Brith Youth Organization, University of Michigan-Ann Arbor Chabad House, Eastern Michigan University Hillel, Temple Israel, Congregation Beth Shalom, and Congregation Beth Isaac for allowing me access to their collections. I would also like to thank Arcadia Publishing for assisting me with publication. While working on this project, I met some very special people who helped me with my work, especially with the locating and identification of suitable photographs. I would like to recognize Jan Durecki, Sharon Alterman, Judy Cantor, Rabbi Jonathan V. Plaut, Rachel Kamin, Rabbi Alter Goldstein, Aaron Kaufman, Jeff Taylor, Arnold Weiner, Wendy Bice, Barbara Barnosky, Marilyn and Fred Krainen, and Anna Wilson. Thank you for helping me with this project!

INTRODUCTION

In 2001, Arcadia Publishing published *Jewish Detroit*, by Irwin Cohen, as part of its Images of America series. Cohen's *Jewish Detroit* focused primarily on Detroit up until the end of World War II. This book is intended to complement Cohen's book by focusing on the most recent six decades of Jewish Detroit. Jewish life in the Metropolitan (Metro) Detroit area for the last 60 years has been about community and family. It came about during the migration to the suburbs during the middle of the 20th century as people sought relief from the congestion and turmoil of the urban center. Many suburbs and neighborhoods within the area serve as bedroom communities. The Jewish community of Metro Detroit is perhaps one of the more diverse in the country in its religious affiliation. Not only are there several congregation of each of the more common movements within Judaism (Reform, Conservative, and Orthodox), but there are also the less common ones (Reconstructionist and Humanistic). Rabbi Sherwin Wine founded the Humanistic movement in Metro Detroit in 1963. Within Detroit's Orthodox community can be found Jews of Ashkenazic, Hasidic, and Sephardic traditions and origins.

The last 60 years of history in Detroit and its environs have seen more change and flux than any other 60-year period within its history. The year 1945 witnessed the end of World War II and the Holocaust. There is not a single Jewish community in the world that was not somehow affected by these events. Detroit's Jews not only participated in the United States war efforts, but also have borne witness to the death of the six million Jews through its more recent Holocaust Museum, built in 1984. Spirits ran high, and hope for a better future was in the air by 1948, when Detroit's economy boomed with the postwar automobile industry, and Israel acquired its independence. However, Jewish Detroit did not remain confined within the city limits with the onset of economic prosperity. As Detroit blossomed in the postwar period, middle and upper class families began trickling to the suburbs to live what was considered the idealized American dream. As the Jews of Detroit moved to the suburbs, they brought with them their congregations and communal institutions. The move from Detroit to the suburbs north of Eight Mile Road was not a Jewish event, but one of socioeconomic class and race. By the 1970s, the trickle had turned into a deluge. The civil rights movement, Israel's wars to maintain independence, and the Cold War left a lasting impression on the Detroit Jewish community from the 1950s into the early 1980s. The Jewish community of Metro Detroit also helped thousands of Jewish Soviet refugees reestablish themselves in Michigan. Due to Metro Detroit's unusual position that straddles an international border, many Jews from the Detroit-Windsor area became involved in Michigan, Ontario, United States, Canadian, and international politics. Notable figures include U.S. senator Carl Levine, Canadian deputy prime minister Herb Gray, and philanthropist Max Fisher. During the 1980s, the Jewish community that had lived in Detroit was entirely scattered throughout the Metro Region, and is now almost nonexistent within Detroit's physical city limits. Farmington Hills, Oak Park, Royal Oak, Southfield, West Bloomfield, and Bloomfield

Hills in Oakland and western Wayne Counties became the new, collective foci of the Jewish community of the metro area with their massive congregations. Smaller congregations can also be found in places like Trenton and Livonia.

Windsor, Canada, is the urban and suburban fabric that extends to the southeast of Detroit even though it is located in a completely separate country, with only the Detroit River separating it. Most of the Canadian Jews in Windsor live closer to downtown Detroit than the Jews of suburban Oakland County, where many of the American Jews of the area reside. Jewish residents of both sides of the border participate in each other's events, such as youth programs and summer camps. Communal ties pass across the Ambassador Bridge and Detroit-Windsor Tunnel, uniting the binational community into a single cultural landscape.

To the west and northwest of Detroit are the cities of Ann Arbor, Flint, and Ypsilanti. Ann Arbor and Flint have their own independently standing Jewish communities. However, due to urban sprawl, these smaller cities have grown and become a part of the Greater Metro Detroit region, and so have their Jewish communities. By including Ann Arbor, Flint, and Ypsilanti, I hope to demonstrate that Jewish life in these areas did not function in a vacuum from the Jews living in Detroit and its suburbs. Flint is an industrial based city whose destiny has been intricately connected with Detroit's for the majority of the 20th century. Ann Arbor is a college town, home of the University of Michigan. According to the University of Michigan Hillel, the Jewish student population comprises an estimated 20 to 25 percent of the student body at the university, many of whom originate from the suburbs adjacent to Detroit. Hillel is a Jewish organization for college students with chapters located all over the world. Over the past couple of decades, many Jewish University of Michigan graduates from the Detroit suburbs have settled in the Ann Arbor area. While Ypsilanti has never had an organized Jewish community, there are a number of Jewish students at Eastern Michigan University who are from the Detroit suburbs and are involved in an active Hillel on that campus. Eastern Michigan University Hillel also falls under the larger umbrella of Hillel of Metro Detroit.

The Greatest Generation of the Detroit Jewish community, who grew up during the Great Depression and participated in World War II, transplanted the community to suburbia. Their children, the baby boomers, shared in this experience as children, either having been born in Detroit and growing up in the suburbs, or were born in the suburbs shortly after their family moved there. The Greatest Generation and the baby boomer generation continued to have a close affiliation with the city during the turmoil of the 1960s and 1970s. The baby boomer generation experienced their earlier years within the city of Detroit and came of age in the suburbs. Therefore, many of this generation have an affinity with Detroit from their experiences there during the third quarter of the 20th century. However, for most of the area's Jewish members of Generation X and Generation Y, their entire saga has been focused almost exclusively in suburbia. It is now possible to live, work, and function exclusively in the suburbs; and this lifestyle differs completely from previous generations of Jewish Detroiters. Bedroom communities have grown into full service communities since places of work and shopping have also relocated from the city to suburbia. Corporate office parks and shopping malls are where most suburban residents commute to today, instead of downtown as they had done before. As Generation X, Generation Y, and the next generation replaces the previous generations, the term Jewish Detroiter will become less and less applicable in a technical sense. This is because the newest generations are strictly suburbanites from birth and their affinity is with suburbia.

The following images are a sampling of the Jewish Community of Metro Detroit since 1945, and are not intended to be comprehensive in any fashion. My intentions are that this book will appeals to a contemporary audience. The representation of what is presented in this book is skewed to the sources available to me, though I did my best to strike an equal balance between secular and religious life (and the entire spectrum in between).

One

JEWISH DETROIT
AFTER THE WAR

On V-J Day, August 12, 1945, Alfred Eisenstadt of *Life* magazine took the famous picture of a sailor kissing a nurse in New York's Time Square. This image has since become an American icon that World War II was finally over and that better times laid ahead. Pictured here is the first kiss of Marilyn and Fred Krainen as husband and wife in Marilyn's childhood home in Detroit. Married in 1951, this image is Jewish Detroit's version of Eisenstadt's picture, signifying that World War II was over and that a whole new way of life was about to begin for Jewish Detroiters. (Courtesy of the private collection of Marilyn and Fred Krainen.)

Marilyn and Fred Krainen are under the chuppah, or wedding canopy, of their wedding with their friends and family surrounding them. (Courtesy of the private collection of Marilyn and Fred Krainen.)

Marilyn Goodman is moments away from becoming Marilyn Krainen and is getting ready for her wedding in her room. (Courtesy of the private collection of Marilyn and Fred Krainen.)

Fred Krainen signs his wedding *ketubah*, or wedding contract. (Courtesy of the private collection of Marilyn and Fred Krainen.)

A newly married couple leaves Temple Beth El in Detroit during the early 1950s. An explosion of weddings in the years following the end of World War II kicked-off the next generation, called the baby boom. (Courtesy of the Leo M. Franklin Archives at Temple Beth El.)

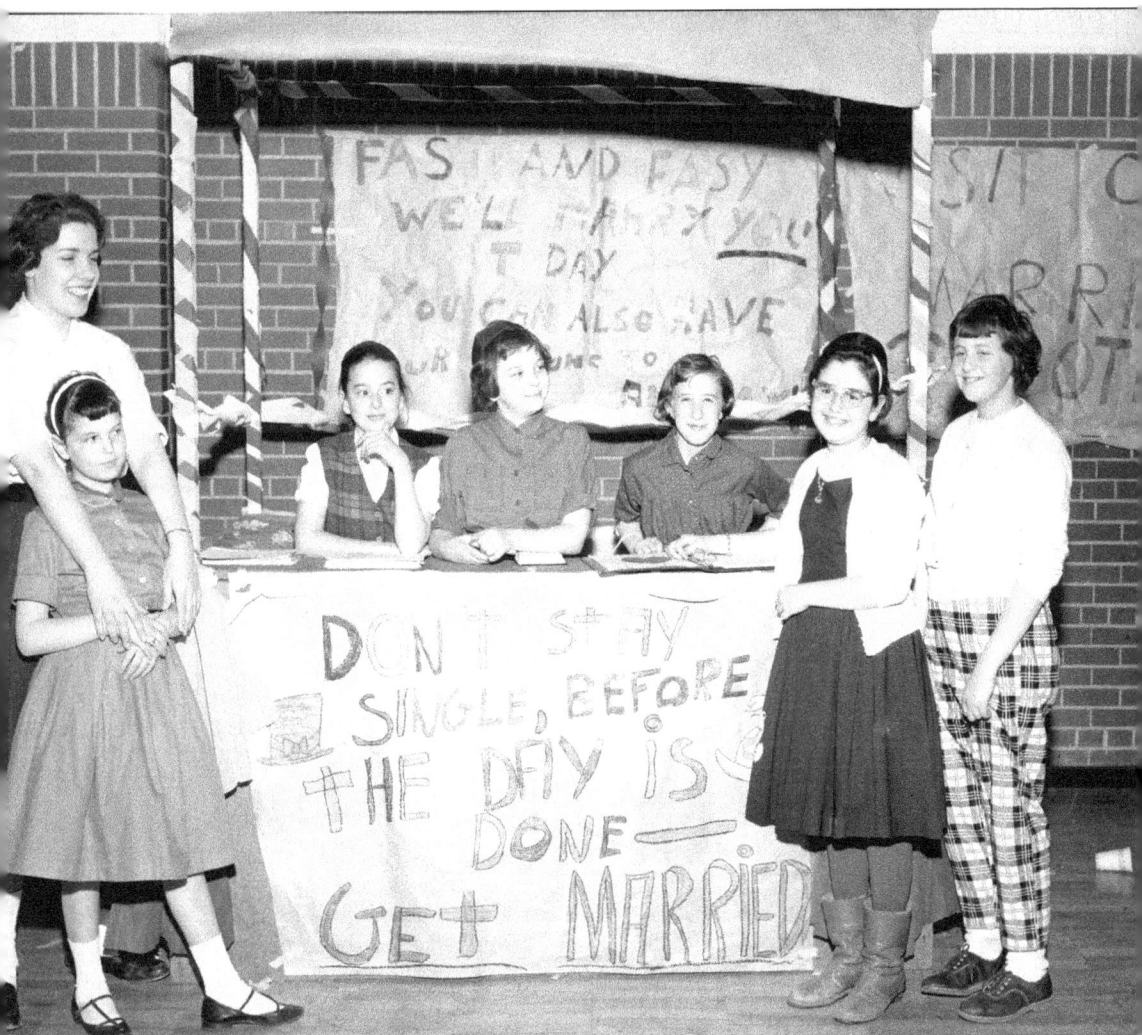

During a Purim celebration in 1958, at the Detroit Jewish Community Center, seven young ladies play a game and poke fun at the wedding craze of the times. Their booth advertises "Don't stay single, before the day is done—Get Married!" and that getting married is "Fast and easy, we'll marry you today." (Courtesy of the Detroit Federation Leonard N. Simons Jewish Community Archives.)

With World War II over in 1945, the Jews of Detroit looked to the future for better times. Here, children of Temple Israel put on a play at the Detroit Institute of Arts, with the theme of having Palestine as the National Jewish Homeland. Little did they know at this time, that within less then three years, Israel declared its independence, thus establishing a national Jewish homeland. (Courtesy of the Detroit Federation Leonard N. Simons Jewish Community Archives.)

Seen here are the winners of Temple Israel's Sukkah Design Contest of 1947 at the Detroit Institute of Arts. Prior to building their first building, the congregation of Temple Israel, during the 1940s, met at the Detroit Institute of Arts. (Courtesy of Temple Israel.)

Two boys put on a demonstration of acrobatics at the Detroit Jewish Community Center Gymnasium. (Courtesy of the Detroit Federation Leonard N. Simons Jewish Community Archives.)

Sports and recreation were a very important experience of growing up. Getting ready for a game is the Temple Beth El basketball team from the late 1950s. (Courtesy of the Leo M. Franklin Archives at Temple Beth El.)

The baby boom created a need for educational opportunities for young children. Here, a young girl is at play on an indoor monkey-bar structure at a Jewish nursery school in Detroit during the 1950s. (Courtesy of the Detroit Federation Leonard N. Simons Jewish Community Archives; photograph by Benyas Kaufman.)

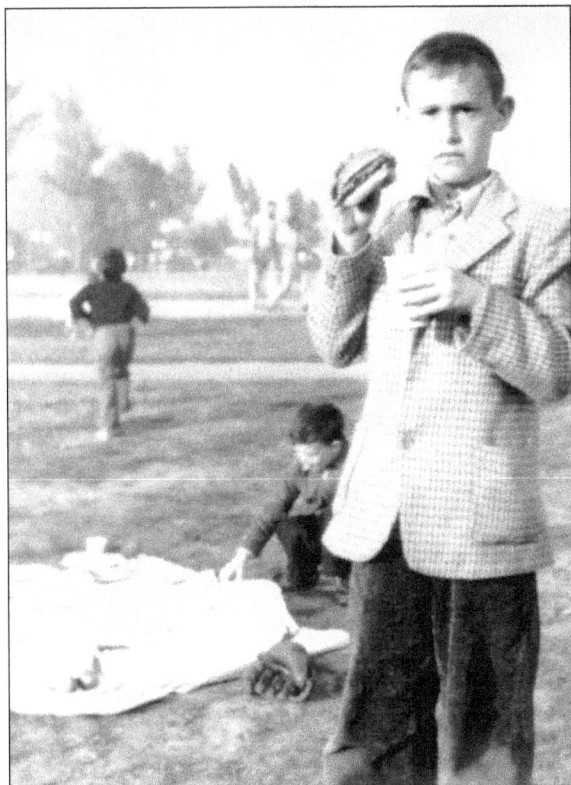

During pleasant weather, families often took their children to parks to play and to picnic. Here, a boy wearing a yarmulke is having a hamburger at a picnic in a Detroit city park. (Courtesy of the Detroit Federation Leonard N. Simons Jewish Community Archives; photograph by Walter Kamn.)

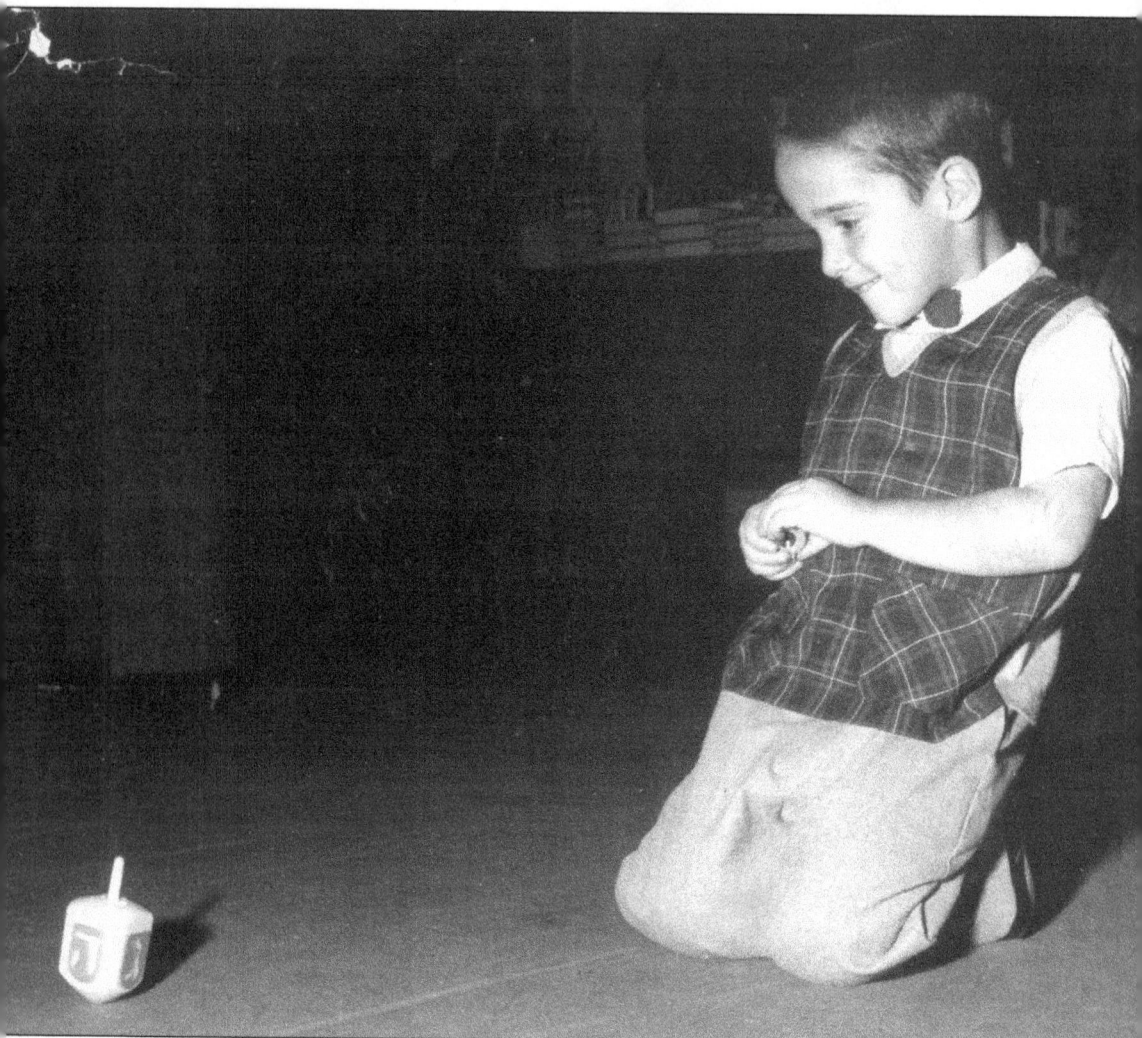

Hanukah is a popular holiday among children because of the presents and games associated with it. Here, a young boy spins his dreidel during Hanukah at nursery school in Detroit during the 1950s. (Courtesy of the Detroit Federation Leonard N. Simons Jewish Community Archives.)

Here, a young girl and her grandfather pose for the camera as they enjoy their time together, sometime in the 1960s. (Courtesy of the Detroit Federation Leonard N. Simons Jewish Community Archives; photograph by Benyas Kaufman.)

Scouting is a non-denominational youth organization that emphasizes the development of proper moral character; including reverence to God. Pictured here is a highly decorated Boy Scout of troop No. 148 of the Detroit Area Council and also a member of Temple Israel during the 1960s. Not only is this scout well decorated with many merit badges, but has earned the prestigious Eagle Scout Award and Ner Tamid Award. The Eagle Scout Award is earned after years of work, including the requirement of organizing a service project that is beneficial to the community at large. The Ner Tamid Award is the Jewish equivalent within scouting, requiring a substantial time commitment to Jewish education and community service. (Courtesy of Temple Israel.)

Playing and having fun is not the sole task for children. Here Mr. Levine plays the violin at the Detroit Jewish Community Center for a small audience of ladies in the background. (Courtesy of the Detroit Federation Leonard N. Simons Jewish Community Archives.)

The Temple Israel confirmation class of 1968 is seen in the sanctuary of Temple Israel in Detroit. (Courtesy of Temple Israel.)

Seen here is the Temple Beth El confirmation class of 1946 in the sanctuary of Temple Beth El in Detroit. The middle section of this picture appears on the front cover of this book, with the full picture appearing here. The famous Detroit Jewish architect and Temple Beth El congregant, Albert Kahn, designed Temple Beth El's building in Detroit on Woodward Avenue and Gladstone Street in the 1920s, and the location was used from 1922 to 1973. "Let There Be Light" is a fitting theme for the spirit of the post-World War II era that the Detroit Jewish community embarked on in 1946. (Courtesy of the Leo M. Franklin Archives at Temple Beth El.)

Listed from left to right, Judge Theodore Levin, Judge Henry Butzel, Max Fisher, and Isidore Sobeloff of the Detroit United Jewish Communities (UJC) Jewish Federation meet to discuss the growth and changes of the Detroit Jewish community. (Courtesy of the Detroit Federation Leonard N. Simons Jewish Community Archives.)

Rabbi Richard Hertz of Temple Beth El is seen here, center, holding a Torah with fellow congregants in Detroit in the 1950s. (Courtesy of the Leo M. Franklin Archives at Temple Beth El.)

Rabbi Benedict Glazer of Temple Beth El was an important rabbi during the middle of the 20th century in Detroit. (Courtesy of the Leo M. Franklin Archives at Temple Beth El.)

Rabbi Louis Finkelstein (left), chancellor of the Jewish Theological Seminary, is seen here, with Rabbi Abraham Hershman (right) and Rabbi Morris Adler of Congregation Shaarey Zedek, in Detroit during the 1960s. (Courtesy of the Shaarey Zedek Archives.)

Rabbi Max Arzt (left), chancellor of the Jewish Theological Seminary, federal Judge Wade McCree (third from left), and Rebbetzin Goldie Adler (second from right), wife of Rabbi Morris Adler, are discussing Detroit community issues at Congregation Shaarey Zedek. (Courtesy of the Shaarey Zedek Archives.)

Michigan governor G. Mennen Williams is seen here signing the Absentee Voters Act in Lansing, in May 1950, permitting voting by absentee ballot when elections conflict with religious holidays; including Jewish holidays. Witnessing the signing are Rabbi Leon Fram of Temple Israel (left), Rabbi Morris Adler of Shaarey Zedek (second from right), and State Senator Charles Blondy (far right). (Courtesy of the Shaarey Zedek Archives.)

At this press conference in the Detroit mayor's office on September 12, 1980, Max Fisher (left), one of Detroit's better-known Jewish philanthropists involved with the project, Detroit mayor Coleman Young (center), and Michigan governor William Milliken speak with reporters on the building of the Riverfront Apartment project. (Courtesy of the Detroit Federation Leonard N. Simons Jewish Community Archives.)

Rabbi Morris Adler of Congregation Shaarey Zedek (right) and Dr. Fidlow, president of Congregation Shaarey Zedek, are seen meeting with former first lady Eleanor Roosevelt during her Israel Bond Drive appearance at Shaarey Zedek in 1956. (Courtesy of the Shaarey Zedek Archives.)

Rabbi Richard Hertz of Temple Beth El talks on Detroit radio station WJR 760AM in the 1950s. (Courtesy of the Leo M. Franklin Archives at Temple Beth El.)

Rabbi Leon Fram of Temple Israel is seen here. (Courtesy of Temple Israel.)

Fred Krainen is seen in Korea at the 38th Parallel during the 1950s. Many expected that World War II would be the war to end all wars. However, like World War I before it, peace was only temporary. After the conclusion of World War II began, the hostile arms race of the Cold War between the United States, and her allies, and the Soviet Union, and its allies, began. Following the call of duty, and at other times the draft, Jewish Detroiters participated in the wars in Korea, Vietnam, and Iraq, as well as other military conflicts that the United States became involved with. (Courtesy of the private collection of Marilyn and Fred Krainen.)

Detroiters rally to support Israel on June 4, 1967, during the Israeli Six-Day War. The military conflicts of the United States were far from the only concerns that were on the minds of many Jewish Detroiters. In 1948, 1956, 1967, and 1973, Israel's hostile neighbors declared formal war, and each time Israel had to defend itself against larger military forces. Jews from throughout the world rallied together to support Israel, and Jews from Detroit were often at the forefront of this support. (Courtesy of the Detroit Federation Leonard N. Simons Jewish Community Archives.)

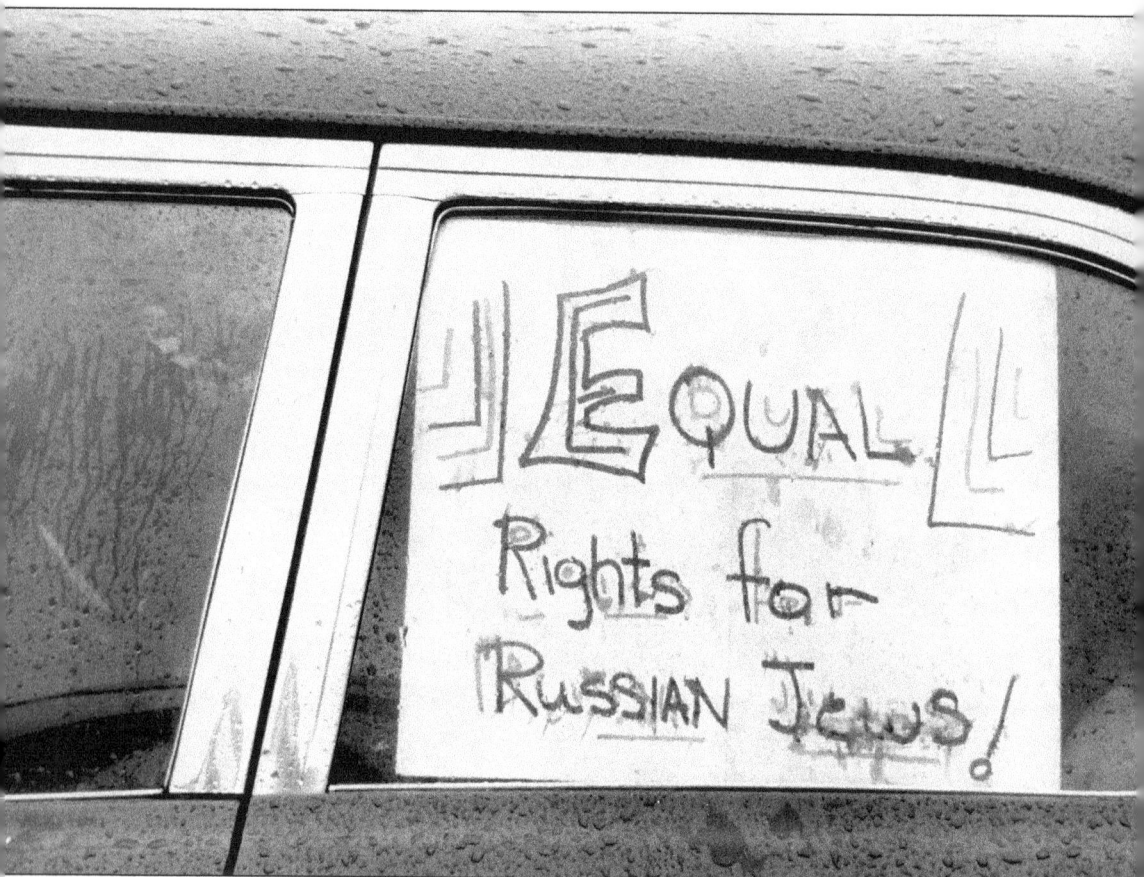

During the 1970s and 1980s, Detroit took in thousands of Jewish refugees from the Soviet Union. The Detroit Jewish community was there to help them and defend their rights. (Courtesy of the Detroit Federation Leonard N. Simons Jewish Community Archives.)

A rally for Jews trapped in the Soviet Union was held in Detroit in April 1972. Young Carl Levin, a future U.S. senator from Michigan, is seated between the words "Let" and "My." (Courtesy of the Detroit Federation Leonard N. Simons Jewish Community Archives.)

Having a connection to Israel has been very important for many Jewish Detroiters. Pictured here is the 1970 class of students who participated in the Detroit Jewish Community Center's Ulpan program in Haifa, Israel. Ulpan is a language immersion program in Israel to teach people modern Hebrew. (Courtesy of the Detroit Federation Leonard N. Simons Jewish Community Archives.)

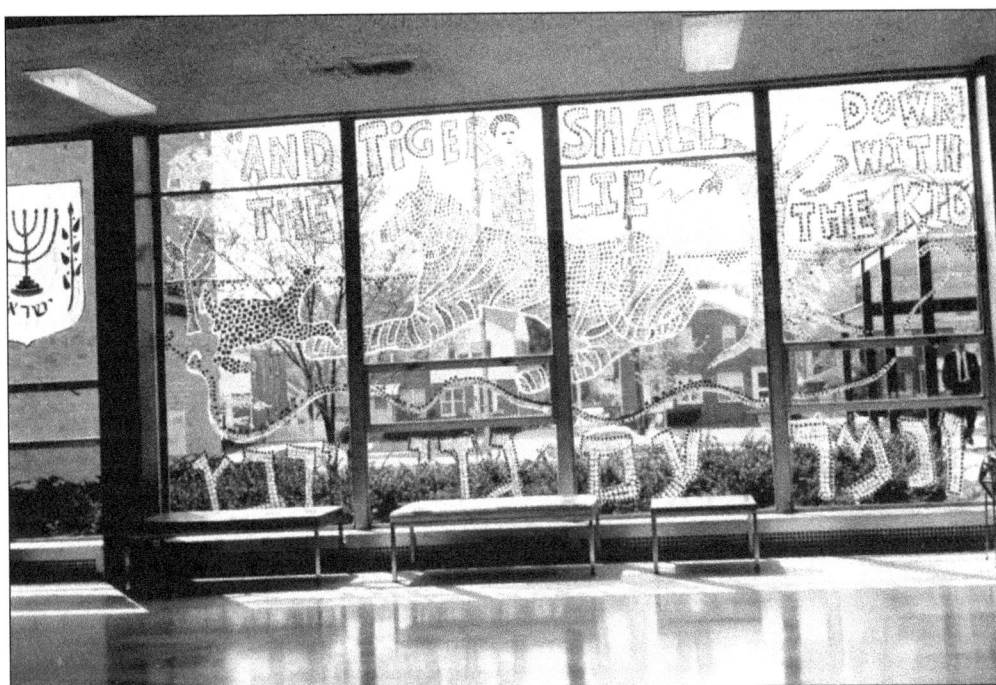

A decorative window mural painted at the Detroit Jewish Community Center from the 1960s is seen here. (Courtesy of the Detroit Federation Leonard N. Simons Jewish Community Archives.)

Sinai Hospital was founded by the Jewish community of Detroit in 1953 and served anyone needing its medical attention. Of particular significance pertaining to Sinai Hospital is that it was the place where many Jewish Detroiters were born. In 1999, Sinai Hospital merged with Grace Hospital to form Sinai-Grace Hospital. (Courtesy of the Detroit Federation Leonard N. Simons Jewish Community Archives.)

Here is Adat Shalom's sanctuary before services in 1956. (Courtesy of the Detroit Federation Leonard N. Simons Jewish Community Archives.)

The Synagogue Ahavat Achim of Detroit is pictured in 1950. (Courtesy of the Detroit Federation Leonard N. Simons Jewish Community Archives.)

Rabbi Leon Fram stands at the future site of the first Temple Israel building in Detroit around 1950. Architect William E. Kapp designed the first Temple Israel building. (Courtesy of Temple Israel.)

World famous architect Minoru Yamasaki demonstrates his model of the new Temple Beth El, to be built in suburban Bloomfield Hills, to Rabbi Richard Hertz and fellow congregants. Based out of Detroit, Yamasaki is most well known for his design of the World Trade Center in New York, which was destroyed by terrorists on September 11, 2001. Coincidentally, the Temple Beth El building of Bloomfield Hills and the World Trade Center were designed by Yamasaki at the same time. (Courtesy of the Leo M. Franklin Archives at Temple Beth El; photograph by Blair Studio.)

Rabbi Morris Adler (center) leads his colleagues and fellow congregants of Shaarey Zedek as they carry the Congregation's 16 Torah scrolls from their older building on Chicago Boulevard in Detroit to their new building on Bell Road, in suburban Southfield. Scenes, such as this one in 1962, marked the transplantation of the Jewish community in Detroit to the suburbs and surrounding metropolitan region. (Courtesy of the Shaarey Zedek Archives.)

Two

LIFE IN THE
SURROUNDING SUBURBS

By 1975 (corresponding to the Hebrew calendar date of 5735), the Jewish community of Detroit had left the Detroit city limits for good and transplanted itself to the suburbs. Pictured here is the laying of the cornerstone for the new Jewish Community Center in West Bloomfield. Detroit Jewish life continues today to take place in the setting of the surrounding suburban municipalities. (Courtesy of the Detroit Federation Leonard N. Simons Jewish Community Archives.)

The Jewish Community Center in West Bloomfield is seen here, shortly after completion. (Courtesy of the Detroit Federation Leonard N. Simons Jewish Community Archives.)

The Jewish Community Center in West Bloomfield is seen in the 1990s after the addition of the first Holocaust Museum building. (Courtesy of the Detroit Federation Leonard N. Simons Jewish Community Archives.)

Seen here is the affixing of the mezuzah at the Samuel Hechtman Jewish Federation Apartment Building dedication in West Bloomfield. (Courtesy of the Detroit Federation Leonard N. Simons Jewish Community Archives.)

The Max M. Fisher Detroit Jewish Federation Building is in Bloomfield Hills. (Courtesy of the Detroit Federation Leonard N. Simons Jewish Community Archives.)

The Meyer L. Prentis Manor, operated by the Jewish Home for the Aged, in Oak Park is a home for many Jewish senior citizens. (Courtesy of the Detroit Federation Leonard N. Simons Jewish Community Archives; photograph by Benyas Kaufman.)

Many of Metro Detroit's Jewish senior citizens live at the Fleischman Residence apartments for the Jewish Home for the Aged in West Bloomfield. (Courtesy of the Detroit Federation Leonard N. Simons Jewish Community Archives.)

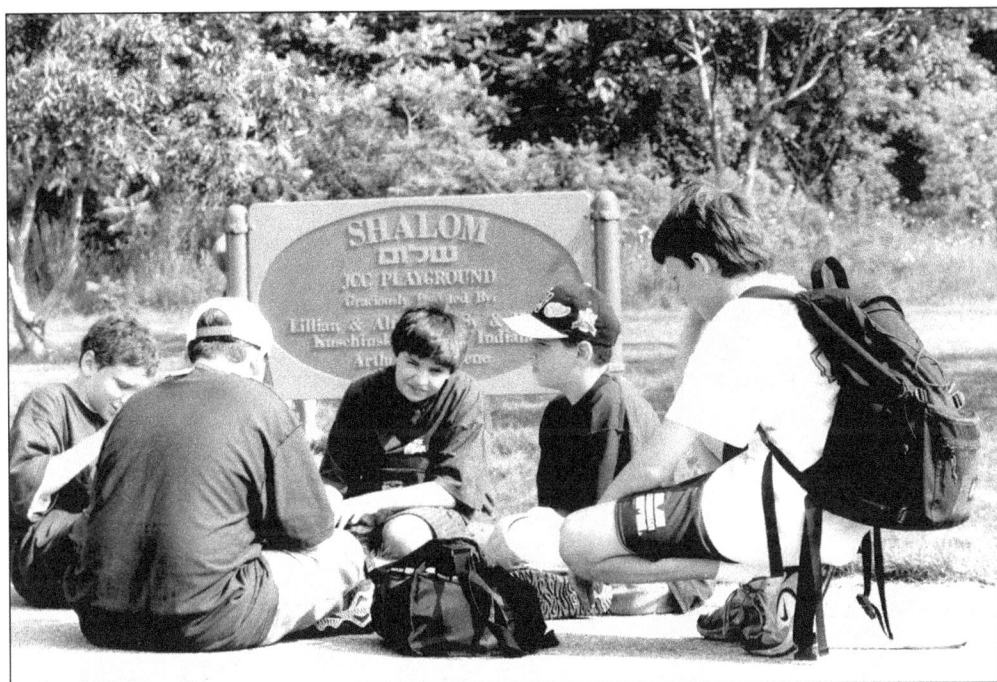

Five boys take it easy at the Shalom Jewish Community Center Playground in West Bloomfield. (Courtesy of the Detroit Federation Leonard N. Simons Jewish Community Archives.)

A family eats lunch together at the kosher cafeteria at the Jewish Community Center. (Courtesy of the Detroit Federation Leonard N. Simons Jewish Community Archives; photograph by Benyas Kaufman.)

The young help the old at the Jewish Home for the Aged in West Bloomfield. (Courtesy of the Detroit Federation Leonard N. Simons Jewish Community Archives.)

The Jewish Community Center in Oak Park hosts an annual Grandparents Day, here in 1987. (Courtesy of the Detroit Federation Leonard N. Simons Jewish Community Archives.)

Residents light Hanukah candles with volunteers at the Jewish Home for the Aged Hechtman Apartments. (Courtesy of the Detroit Federation Leonard N. Simons Jewish Community Archives.)

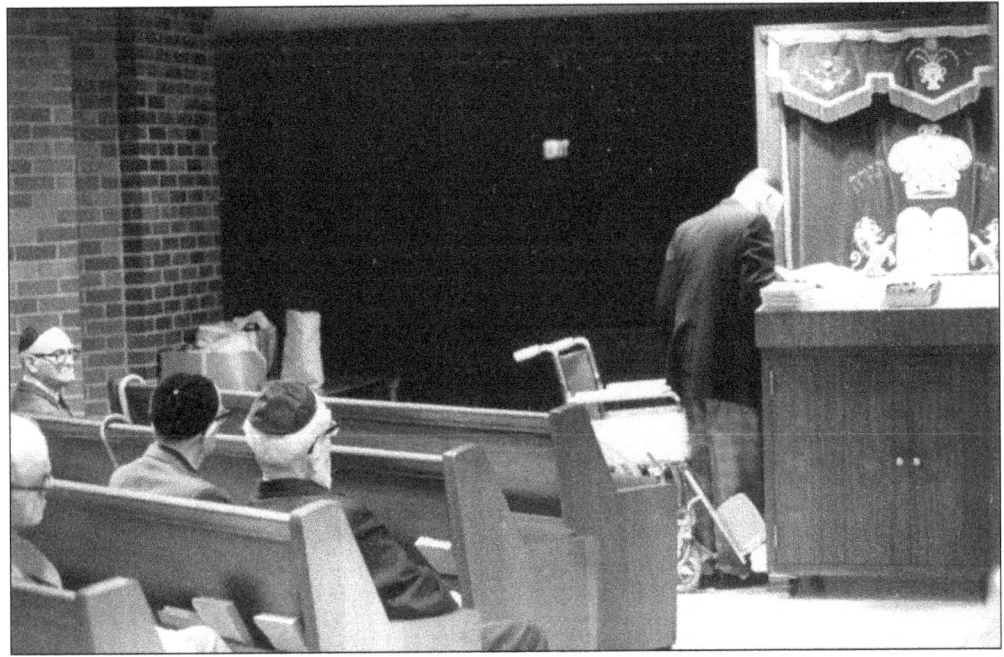

Pictured here is a minyan (a quorum of 10 Jewish adults required for a religious services) of residents worshiping together at the Jewish Home for the Aged Chapel in West Bloomfield. (Courtesy of the Detroit Federation Leonard N. Simons Jewish Community Archives.)

Pictured are the 1978 honored employees who worked at the Jewish Home for the Aged in West Bloomfield. (Courtesy of the Detroit Federation Leonard N. Simons Jewish Community Archives; photograph by Benyas Kaufman.)

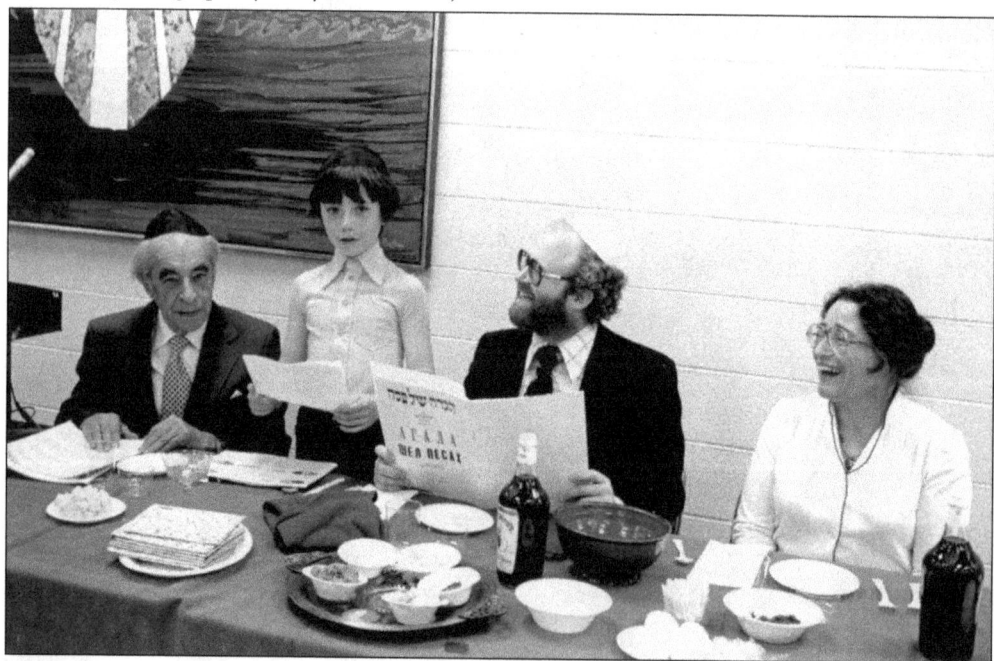

Pictured here are Soviet Jewish refugees at the Jewish Community Center Acculturation Passover Seder. Events like this one, in 1980, were held for Jewish refugees from the Soviet Union to help them adjust to life in the Metro Detroit area, as well as expose to them Jewish religious and cultural activities that had been forbidden to them in the Soviet Union. (Courtesy of the Detroit Federation Leonard N. Simons Jewish Community Archives.)

Swim coach Joel Jacobs is pictured with swimmers at the Jewish Community Center Summer Day Camp in Oak Park. (Courtesy of the Detroit Federation Leonard N. Simons Jewish Community Archives.)

Pictured here are day campers rushing to board the bus for their daily field trips from the Jewish Community Center in Oak Park in the summer of 1973. (Courtesy of the Detroit Federation Leonard N. Simons Jewish Community Archives.)

Children and teachers of the United Hebrew School of Southfield play together in a circle before getting on the bus. (Courtesy of the Detroit Federation Leonard N. Simons Jewish Community Archives.)

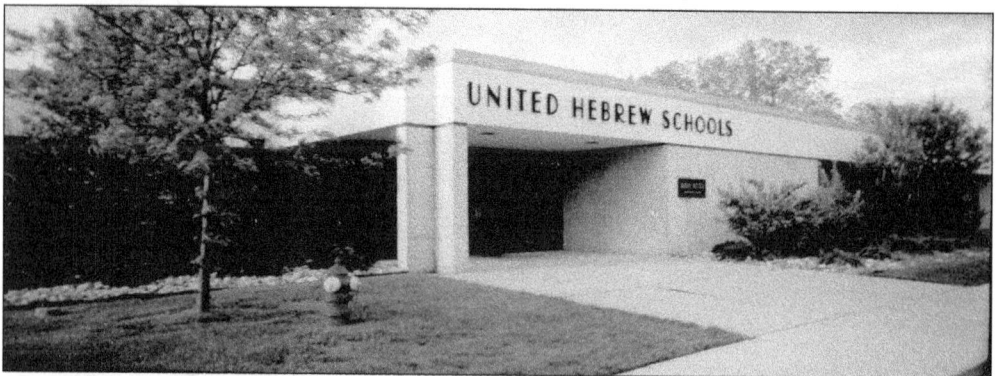

The United Hebrew School building in Southfield is seen here. (Courtesy of the Detroit Federation Leonard N. Simons Jewish Community Archives; photograph by Benyas Kaufman.)

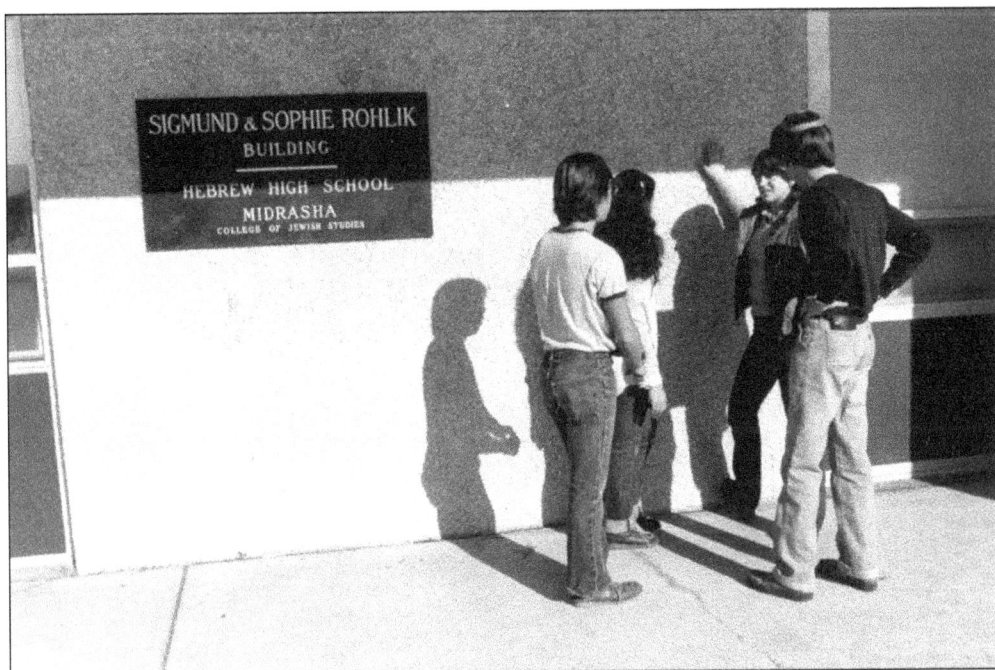

A group of students are seen hanging out after class at the Hebrew High School, Midrasha College of Jewish Studies in Southfield in 1980. (Courtesy of the Detroit Federation Leonard N. Simons Jewish Community Archives; photograph by Benyas Kaufman.)

Rabbi Sherwin Wine is teaching a class to Jewish senior citizens in Birmingham. Rabbi Wine was involved in founding the Humanistic Movement in Judaism in suburban Detroit in 1963. Humanistic Judaism strives to offer a nontheistic alternative in contemporary Jewish life with congregations in the United States, Canada, Israel, and many other parts of the world. Prior to 1963, Rabbi Wine serviced the congregation Temple Beth El in Windsor, Canada. (Courtesy of the Detroit Federation Leonard N. Simons Jewish Community Archives.)

A young girl at the United Hebrew Schools learns about charity with the tzedaka box she is holding and Shabbat with the candle sticks, kiddish cup, and covered challah in front of her in 1981. (Courtesy of the Detroit Federation Leonard N. Simons Jewish Community Archives.)

Challah rolls and juice are served as snack at the United Hebrew Schools in Southfield in 1981. (Courtesy of the Detroit Federation Leonard N. Simons Jewish Community Archives.)

A B'nai Brith Girl (BBG) holds a havdala candle during the havdala service that marks the end of Shabbat. The B'nai Brith Youth Organization (BBYO) is an organization for high school age men and women. The Michigan Region of BBYO, based out of the Jewish Community Center in West Bloomfield, is one of the largest regions within the international organization. The Michigan Region of BBYO encompasses all of the Metro Detroit area; including the Detroit suburbs, Ann Arbor, and Windsor, Canada. (Courtesy of Arnold Weiner, Michigan Region of BBYO.)

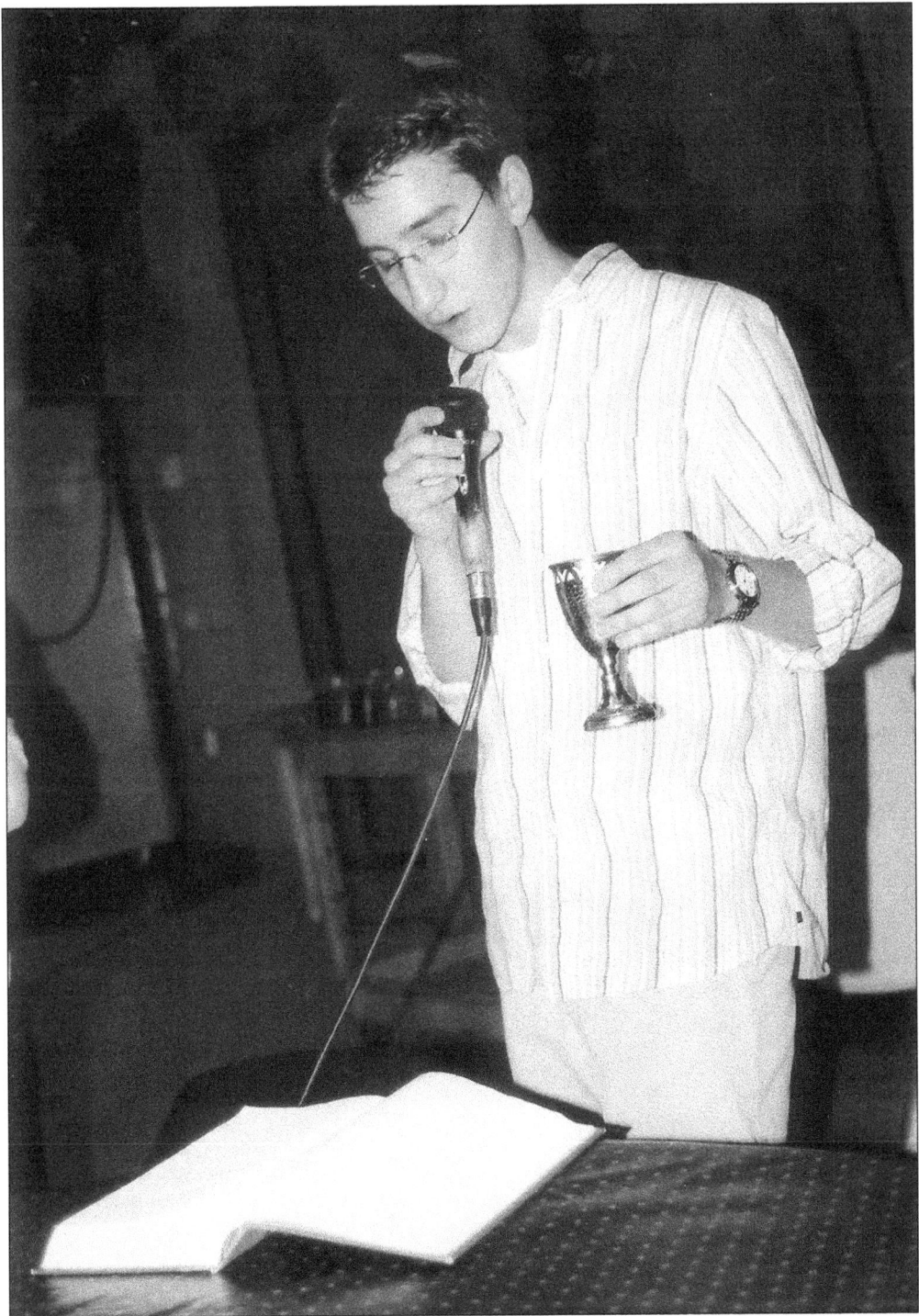

The men's group within BBYO is known as Aleph Zadik Aleph (AZA). Pictured here is a young man holding a kiddish cup while reciting the prayers for the havdala service at a BBYO function in suburban Detroit. AZA is the men's division of BBYO, whereas BBG is the women's division. (Courtesy of Arnold Weiner, Michigan Region of BBYO.)

The BBYO visits the new Holocaust Museum in Farmington Hills to learn about this terrible period in Jewish history. (Courtesy of Arnold Weiner, Michigan Region of BBYO.)

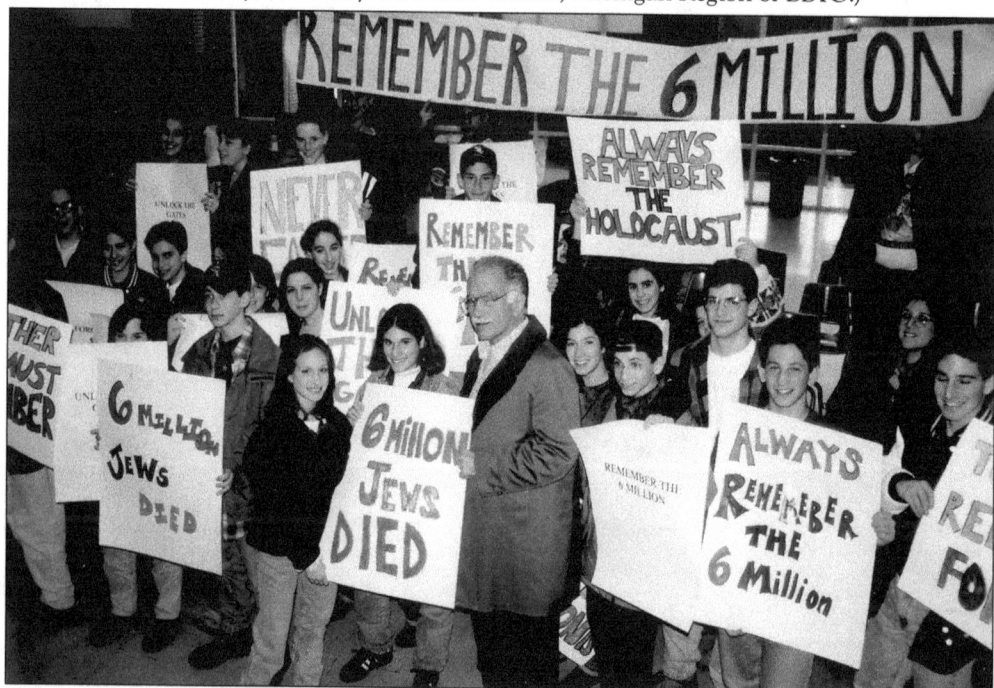

The BBYO puts on a rally to spread awareness of the Holocaust and to remember the six million Jews who died in Nazi-occupied Europe during the 1930s and 1940s. Remembering the lessons of the Holocaust is important for preventing acts of human genocide from occurring again in the future. (Courtesy of Arnold Weiner, Michigan Region of BBYO.)

BBYO volunteers work with Habitat for Humanity to build and repair homes for those who are unable to afford to. *Tzedaka*, the giving or providing of charity, is considered an important part of living a Jewish life. (Courtesy of Arnold Weiner, Michigan Region of BBYO.)

BBYO volunteers work at a food bank to help feed the poor of Detroit. (Courtesy of Arnold Weiner, Michigan Region of BBYO.)

In 2004, Jewish Americans from across the United States celebrated the 350th anniversary of a Jewish presence on the North American continent. The first Jews to settle in what became the United States arrived by ship in New York (then New Amsterdam) in 1654. The Michigan Region of BBYO celebrated this anniversary with a giant cake. (Courtesy of Arnold Weiner, Michigan Region of BBYO.)

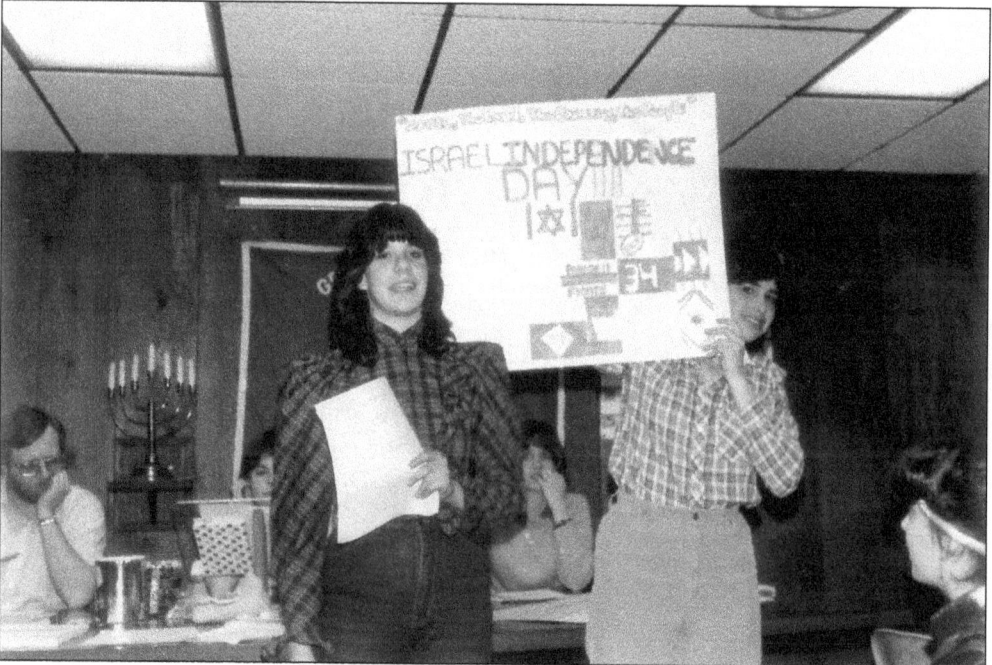

The BBYO celebrates Israel's independence in 1982. (Courtesy of Arnold Weiner, Michigan Region of BBYO.)

58

In 1999, BBYO celebrated its 75th anniversary. That same year was Arnold Weiner's 30th year as Michigan regional director. After over 30 years of dedicated service to Metro Detroit Jewish youth in Michigan and Ontario, Arnold Weiner has touched the lives of an entire generation of members within the greater community. (Courtesy of Michigan Region of BBYO.)

Posing for a goofy picture in a canoe are the 2005 Michigan Region of BBYO staff and advisors. (Courtesy of Arnold Weiner, Michigan Region of BBYO.)

Michigan Region of BBYO representatives display their banner for the 2003 Regional Convention. The theme for the convention was "a great miracle happened here." (Courtesy of Arnold Weiner, Michigan Region of BBYO.)

Members of BBYO are putting on a comic routine parody, called JewSync, at one of their regular region wide events. (Courtesy of Arnold Weiner, Michigan Region of BBYO.)

AZA members of BBYO are showing off their hidden talents in a show at their annual regional event. (Courtesy of Arnold Weiner, Michigan Region of BBYO.)

Jewish college students have fun at Havdala Replugged, sponsored by Hillel of Metro Detroit. Hillel is an international Jewish student organization with chapters on college campuses with a significant Jewish presence. Both BBYO and Hillel were once part of B'nai Brith International, so high school students involved with BBYO often become involved with Hillel. Hillel of Metro Detroit serves Jewish students at colleges and universities within the Metro Detroit area. (Courtesy of Hillel of Metro Detroit; photograph by Karen Adelman.)

An athlete from Detroit shows off this medal that he has just won at the Maccabi Games in Pittsburgh, Pennsylvania, around 1985. (Courtesy of Temple Israel.)

Arina Bourmistova from Russia performs at the Neighborhood Project Concert in Oak Park to help raise funds and awareness for community service projects. (Courtesy of the Detroit Federation Leonard N. Simons Jewish Community Archives; photograph by Glen Trist.)

The Avodah Dance Ensemble performs around 1980. (Courtesy of Temple Israel.)

At the Temple Israel in West Bloomfield dedication in 1989, a group of children are having fun in a bin of balls that are part of the festivities. (Courtesy of Temple Israel.)

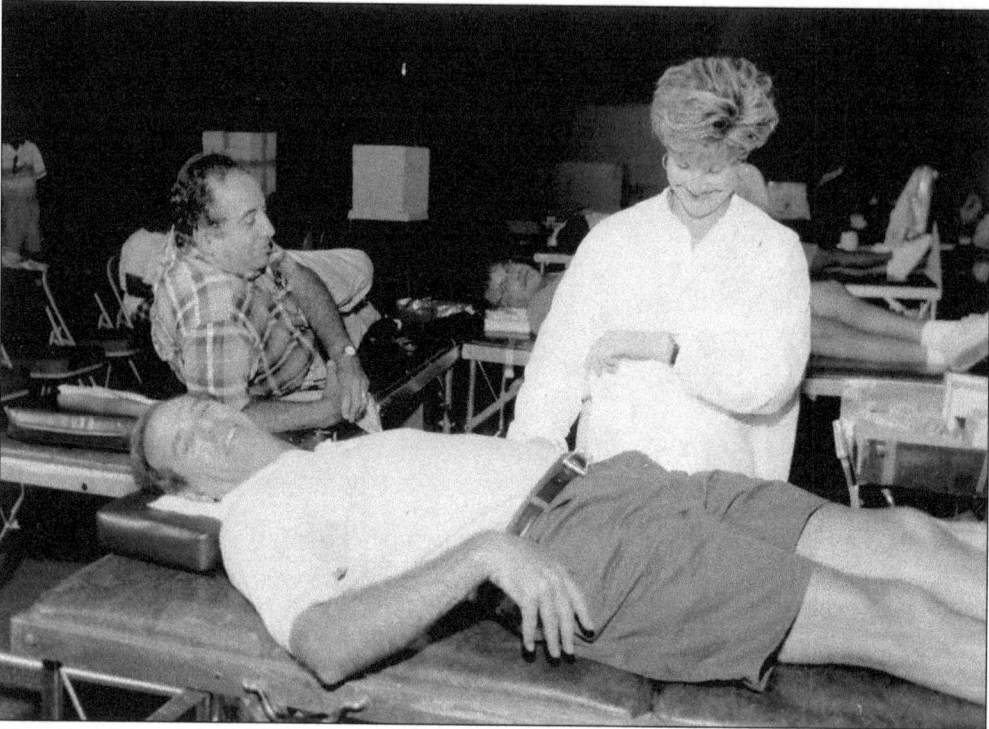

This 1995 Temple Israel blood drive benefited the American Red Cross in West Bloomfield. (Courtesy of Temple Israel.)

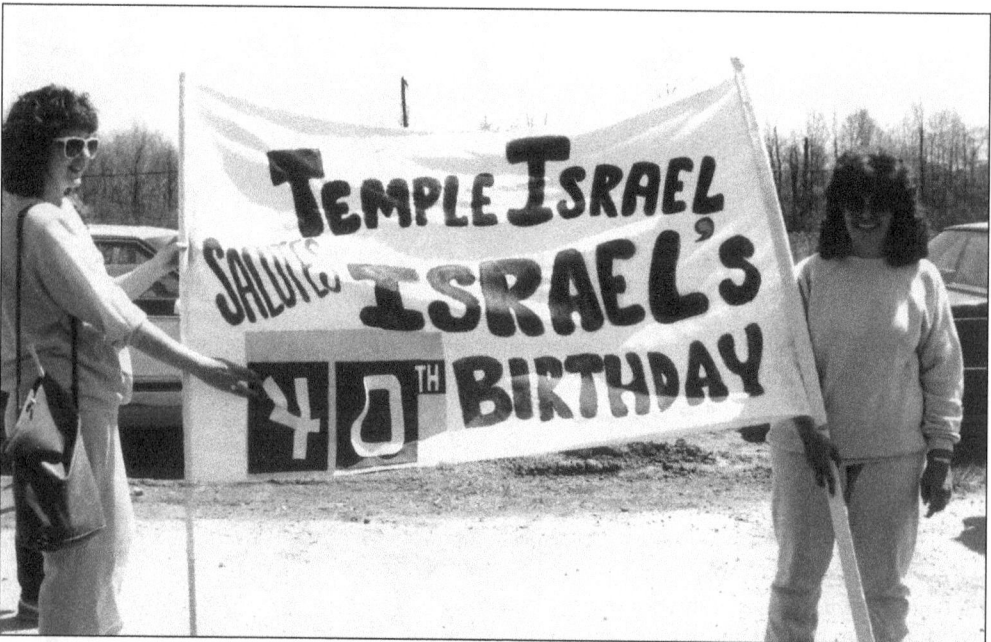

Temple Israel celebrates Israel's 40th anniversary of independence in 1988 in West Bloomfield. (Courtesy of Temple Israel.)

Leslie Schmier and Temple Israel parade with the Torahs as they celebrate the holiday of Simchat Torah. (Courtesy of Temple Israel.)

This architect's rendering was drawn up for the Temple Israel building in West Bloomfield. (Courtesy of Temple Israel.)

Architect Percival Goodman designed this 1962 model of the Shaarey Zedek synagogue in Southfield. (Courtesy of the Shaarey Zedek Archives.)

The Synagogue Shaarey Zedek in Southfield is pictured shortly after it was built. (Courtesy of the Detroit Federation Leonard N. Simons Jewish Community Archives.)

This Michigan Historical Marker at the Shaarey Zedek synagogue tells about the history of the congregation prior to moving to Southfield in 1962. According to the plaque, the synagogue building in Southfield is the congregation's sixth location since its founding. (Courtesy of the Shaarey Zedek Archives.)

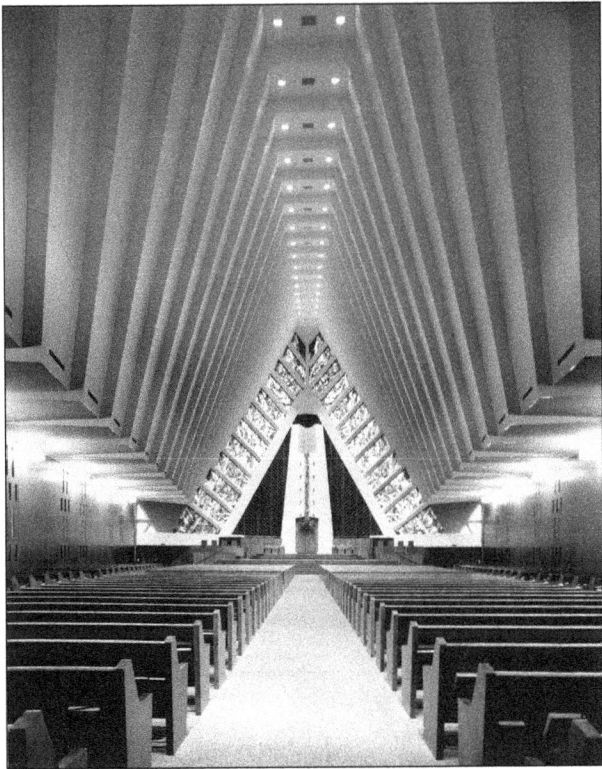

Here is a peek at the architectural beauty of Shaarey Zedek's sanctuary in Southfield. (Courtesy of the Shaarey Zedek Archives.)

Rabbi Irwin Groner welcomes a full house in the Shaarey Zedek sanctuary just prior to the Weisberg concert. (Courtesy of the Shaarey Zedek Archives.)

The Shaarey Zedek B'nai Israel Center is pictured. (Courtesy of the Shaarey Zedek Archives.)

Rabbi Irwin Groner is pictured with Jewish immigrants from the Soviet Union in the Shaarey Zedek sukkah in 1979. Because religious expression in the Soviet Union was oppressed, this was the first time many of these immigrants experienced Sukkot holiday related activities. (Courtesy of the Shaarey Zedek Archives; photograph by Benyas Kaufman.)

Rabbi Irwin Groner and children are pictured at a Seyum Ha-Torah, a special ceremony when the final letters are written to complete the Torah scroll. Authentic Torahs scrolls are still handmade and written by scribes on parchment today as they have traditionally been for thousands of years. (Courtesy of the Shaarey Zedek Archives.)

From left to right are unknown, Sexton Jacob Epel, Mr. and Mrs. Levin, cantor Jacob Sonenklar, and Rabbi Irwin Groner after signing the ketubah, or wedding contract, prior to the Levin's wedding at Shaarey Zedek. (Courtesy of the Shaarey Zedek Archives; photograph by Candid-Art.)

Rabbi Irwin Groner introduces himself to new Jewish immigrants from the Soviet Union in 1969. (Courtesy of the Shaarey Zedek Archives.)

Cantor Chaim Najman is pictured with Yale Levin and son at the son's bar mitzvah at Shaarey Zedek. (Courtesy of the Shaarey Zedek Archives.)

Cantor Sidney Rube is pictured with U.S. senator Carl Levin, cantor Chaim Najman, Harold Berry, president Harvey Weisberg, Louis Berry, Rabbi Irwin Groner, federal Judge Avern Cohn, and William Davidson at Shaarey Zedek's 120th anniversary celebration in 1981. (Courtesy of the Shaarey Zedek Archives.)

Concerts, such as this one, are sometimes played in the Temple Beth El sanctuary. (Courtesy of the Leo M. Franklin Archives at Temple Beth El.)

Pictured here is the exterior of Temple Beth El in Bloomfield Hills. (Courtesy of the Leo M. Franklin Archives at Temple Beth El.)

Standing on the rear side of Temple Beth El is a Michigan Historical Marker providing some history on the congregation. According to the plaque, Temple Beth El moved to the Detroit suburb of Bloomfield Hills because many of its congregants had already moved to the area. The building was built in 1973 and was designed by Minoru Yamasaki, the same architect who designed the World Trade Center in New York. (Courtesy of the Leo M. Franklin Archives at Temple Beth El.)

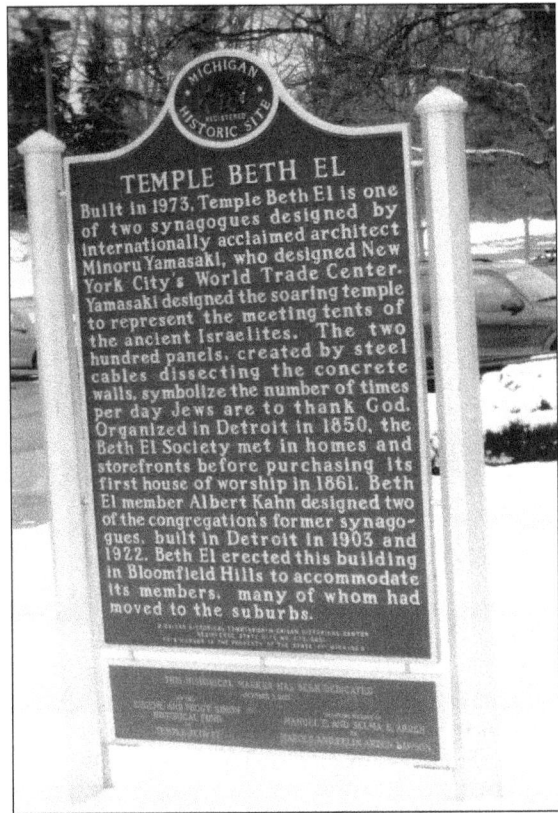

Pictured here is the skeleton frame of Temple Beth El's sanctuary under construction in 1972. (Courtesy of the Leo M. Franklin Archives at Temple Beth El.)

This view welcomes those walking into the sanctuary of Temple Beth El. (Courtesy of the Leo M. Franklin Archives at Temple Beth El.)

The architect, Minoru Yamasaki, designed the interior of the sanctuary of Temple Beth El to appear like the inside of a giant tent. The concept for the tent idea was inspired by the Tabernacle that was a tent used as a house of worship by the biblical Israelites before King Solomon built the First Temple. (Courtesy of the Leo M. Franklin Archives at Temple Beth El.)

Rabbi Morton Kanter is pictured with his family at the groundbreaking for Temple Beth El in Bloomfield Hills in 1972. (Courtesy of the Leo M. Franklin Archives at Temple Beth El.)

Temple Beth El's Boy Scout Troop gets together for a group picture. (Courtesy of the Leo M. Franklin Archives at Temple Beth El.)

Rabbi Alan Meyerowitz is pictured at Congregation B'nai Moshe in Oak Park in the early 1990s. (Courtesy of the Detroit Federation Leonard N. Simons Jewish Community Archives.)

Rabbi Moses Lehrman of Congregation B'nai Moshe in Oak Park supervises Gilbert Stiefel signing a wedding contract before Stiefel's wedding in 1970. (Courtesy of the private collection of Gilbert Stiefel.)

Guests watch a wedding ceremony under the chuppah at Congregation B'nai Moshe in Oak Park in 1970. (Courtesy of the private collection of Gilbert Stiefel.)

The Congregation Beth Shalom in Oak Park is pictured. (Courtesy of the Beth Shalom Archives.)

Morning minyan services of Congregation Beth Shalom were captured in this photograph during a brotherhood retreat in the 1970s. (Courtesy of the Beth Shalom Archives.)

Children at Congregation Beth Shalom celebrate the holiday of Sukkot with a *lulav*, or "palm branch," and etrog, a citrus fruit native to Israel, during the early 1960s. (Courtesy of the Beth Shalom Archives.)

A bar mitzvah student proudly carries the Torah in 1981 at United Hebrew Schools in Southfield. (Courtesy of the Detroit Federation Leonard N. Simons Jewish Community Archives; photograph by Benyas Kaufman.)

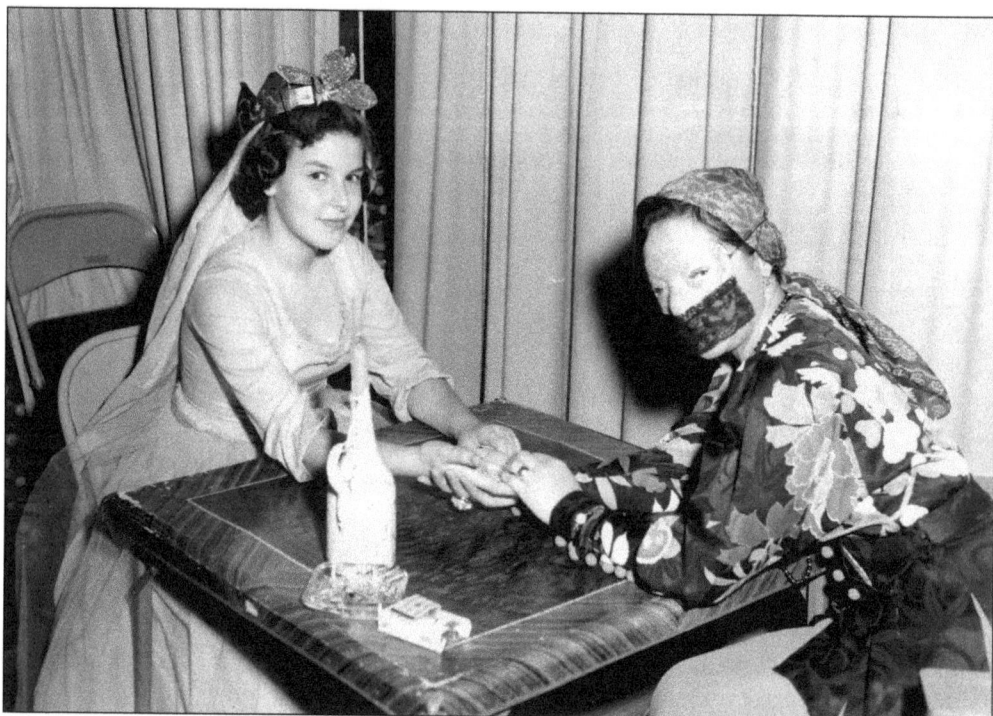

Children in the 1950s at Temple Beth Jacob in Pontiac play games at the annual Purim Party. (Courtesy of the Leo M. Franklin Archives at Temple Beth El.)

A Temple Beth Jacob confirmation class poses for a group picture during the 1980s with Rabbi Richard Weiss in Pontiac. (Courtesy of the Leo M. Franklin Archives at Temple Beth El.)

A Jewish family shows that they have moved into their new home in Oak Park by hanging a mezuzah on their front door post in 1990. (Courtesy of the Detroit Federation Leonard N. Simons Jewish Community Archives.)

The Goodman family poses for a family picture at James Goodman's bar mitzvah during the early 1960s. (Courtesy of the private collection of Barry Stiefel.)

Morris Lapin holds his new grandson while his son-in-law lights the Hanukah candles on the second night at their home in Southfield in 1979. (Courtesy of the private collection of Barry Stiefel.)

Beth Isaac Synagogue in Trenton is pictured here. (Courtesy of the Congregation Beth Isaac; photograph by Barbara Barnosky.)

This is one of several decorative mosaics with Jewish themes that hang in the social hall of Beth Isaac Synagogue. (Courtesy of the Congregation Beth Isaac; photograph by Barbara Barnosky.)

In the rear of Beth Isaac Synagogue's sanctuary hangs a charred Star of David from the first Beth Isaac Synagogue built in 1964. This is all that remains of the first building after it was set on fire by anti-Semitic arsonists in 1967. The second building was built shortly after the fire, and the charred Star of David from the first building hangs in the sanctuary of the second as a reminder that there is anti-Semitism in the Metro Detroit area. (Courtesy of the Congregation Beth Isaac; photograph by Barbara Barnosky.)

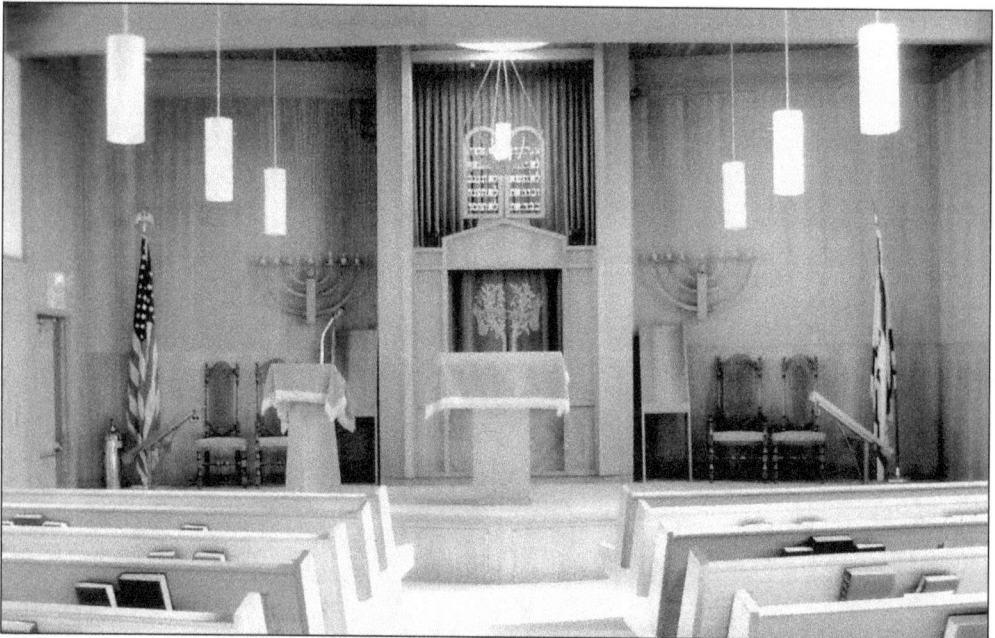

Beth Isaac Synagogue has a small, but very close-knit congregation, as can be seen by the size of the sanctuary. (Courtesy of the Congregation Beth Isaac; photograph by Barbara Barnosky.)

Max Fisher (left), a Jewish philanthropist from Detroit, collects a donation from his friend, Henry Ford II, for the Allied Jewish Campaign to support Israel. (Courtesy of the Detroit Federation Leonard N. Simons Jewish Community Archives.)

Max Fisher (left) meets with Yitzhak Rabin on October 25, 1977, during his trip to Detroit. Yitzhak Rabin was prime minister of Israel twice; his first term from 1974 to 1977, and his second from 1992 to 1995. His second term ended due to an assassination in Tel Aviv. Max Fisher and Yitzhak Rabin had come to know each other during the Israeli Six-Day War in 1967. Max Fisher had been involved in raising funds for the Israeli Defense Forces while Lt. Gen. Yitzhak Rabin was commanding. (Courtesy of the Detroit Federation Leonard N. Simons Jewish Community Archives.)

Max Fisher (right) meets with Israeli Prime Minister Menachem Begin in Detroit in 1981. Menachem Begin succeeded Yitzhak Rabin as prime minister of Israel in 1977 until he resigned after the death of his wife in 1982. (Courtesy of the Detroit Federation Leonard N. Simons Jewish Community Archives.)

U.S. senator Carl Levin of Michigan meets with Shimon Perez. Shimon Perez has been part of Israeli national politics for decades and was prime minister of Israel from 1984 to 1986, and briefly in 1995, following Prime Minister Yitzhak Rabin's assassination. Carl Levin is a native Jewish Detroiter and was the general counsel for the Michigan Civil Rights Commission from 1964 through 1967. He has been in the U.S. senate since 1979. (Courtesy of the Detroit Federation Leonard N. Simons Jewish Community Archives.)

Three

LIFE SOUTH OF THE DETROIT RIVER

WINDSOR

An international border between the United States and Canada divides Detroit from Windsor. The Detroit River marks this border. The Detroit-Windsor border crossing is one of the few places where one goes south into Canada or north into the United States. Though divided by nationality and a river, the Jews of both sides form the cohesive community of Jewish Metro Detroit. Many of Windsor's Jews actually live geographically closer to the city of Detroit then those who live in the northern suburbs on the American half. Pictured above is the Great Lakes Council B'nai Brith Youth Organization (BBYO) 1961 Conclave, with participants from Windsor and Michigan. The Michigan Region of BBYO is an example of a number of Metro Detroit Jewish organizations that bring together members from both sides of the border on a regular basis, thus maintaining the binational dimension of the community. Michigan region's jurisdiction within BBYO includes the entire state of Michigan and Essex County, Ontario, where Windsor is located. (Courtesy of Rabbi Jonathan V. Plaut; photograph by the Windsor Star.)

Michigan and Canadian BBYO members meet outside on a sunny afternoon at the Charles and Florence Milan Camp in Bell River, Ontario. (Courtesy of Arnold Weiner, Michigan Region of BBYO.)

Michigan and Canadian BBYO members pose for a picture in front of the Conference Center (or Centre) at the Charles and Florence Milan BBYO Camp in Bell River, Ontario. (Courtesy of Arnold Weiner, Michigan Region of BBYO.)

Pictured are, from left to right, Rabbi Shmaryuhu Karelitz of Shaarey Zedek, Senator David A. Croll, Rabbi Dr. Samuel S. Stollman of Shaar Hashomayim, and Morris Tabachnick, president of the Windsor Jewish Community Council, at the contributors' banquet for the new Windsor Shaarey Zedek Synagogue that was being built in 1957. (Courtesy of Rabbi Jonathan V. Plaut; photograph by the Windsor Star.)

Pictured here from left to right are Sara Kirzner, Margaret Savage, and Helen Raphael of Hadassah Wizo, promoting a blood drive with the Windsor Red Cross at their bazaar on May 27, 1970. (Courtesy of Rabbi Jonathan V. Plaut; photograph by the Windsor Star.)

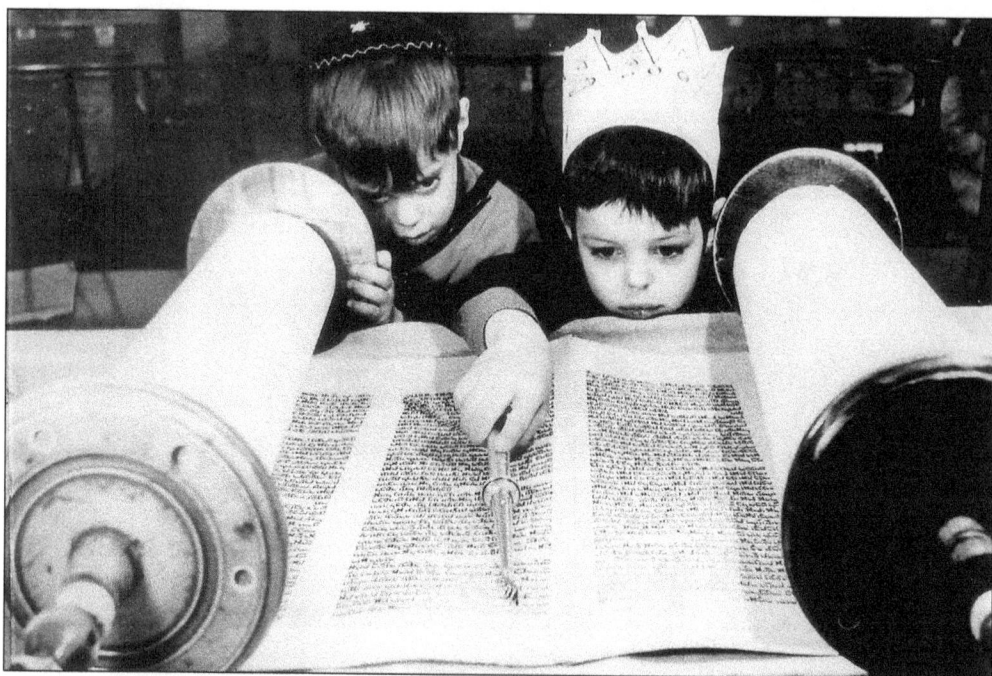

Kevin Smulowitz and his brother Neil examine the Torah during a Purim celebration on February 29, 1972. Kevin and Neil are the sons of Rabbi Hillel Smulowitz of Shaarey Zedek in Windsor. (Courtesy of Rabbi Jonathan V. Plaut; photograph by the Windsor Star.)

The sisterhood at Shaar Hashomayim prepare for the upcoming holiday of Passover by inventorying the received shipment of matzo. Passover is a holiday that remembers the exodus from Egypt of the ancient Israelites, and eating unleavened bread, called matzo, is a tradition that dates back to this time period. (Courtesy of Rabbi Jonathan V. Plaut; photograph by the Windsor Star.)

Mrs. Solovich (left) the past Canadian national president of B'nai Brith and Dorthy Bornstein announce the 1967 annual donor luncheon for the Windsor Chapter of B'nai Brith. (Courtesy of Rabbi Jonathan V. Plaut; photograph by the Windsor Star.)

Myer Dorn (left) and Monty Pomm announce the Windsor Jewish Community Council's celebration of Israel's 10th anniversary of independence in 1958. Israel's 10th anniversary was celebrated on both sides of the border of Metro Detroit's Jewish community. (Courtesy of Rabbi Jonathan V. Plaut; photograph by the Windsor Star.)

Pictured here is the Windsor Jewish Community Centre Building and I. L. Peretz House. The Peretz House is a full-service apartment building for Windsor senior citizens. (Courtesy of Rabbi Jonathan V. Plaut.)

Congregation Beth El of Windsor is pictured here. (Courtesy of Rabbi Jonathan V. Plaut.)

Congregation Shaarey Zedek of Windsor is pictured. (Courtesy of Rabbi Jonathan V. Plaut.)

Congregation Shaar Hashomayim of Windsor is pictured. (Courtesy of Rabbi Jonathan V. Plaut.)

Rabbi Jonathan V. Plaut (right) is pictured with Gerald Freed, a member of the Order of Canada and resident Windsor Jewish native. The Order of Canada is Canada's highest civilian honor (or honour) with membership awarded to those who contribute to making a difference in Canada. (Courtesy of Rabbi Jonathan V. Plaut.)

Rabbi Jonathan V. Plaut (left) meets with Menachem Begin around 1976 in Windsor during a binational trip to the United States and Canada shortly before he became prime minister of Israel. (Courtesy of Rabbi Jonathan V. Plaut.)

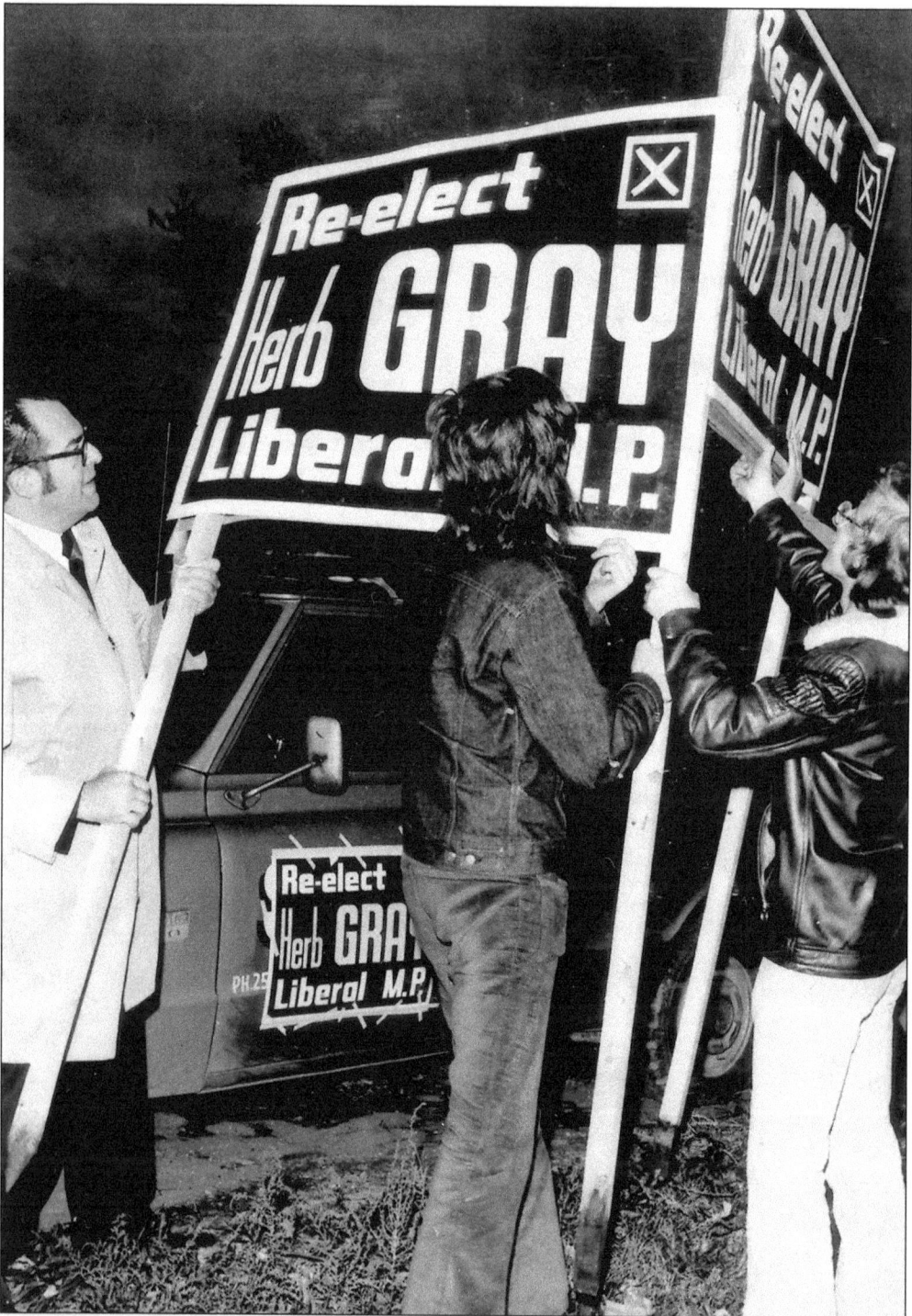

Herb Gray (left) works with committed volunteers on his reelection campaign in 1972, as the Liberal party candidate to Canada's Parliament. Herb Gray is a Windsor native and became Canada's first Jewish deputy prime minister from 1997 to 2002. (Courtesy of Rabbi Jonathan V. Plaut; photograph by the Windsor Star.)

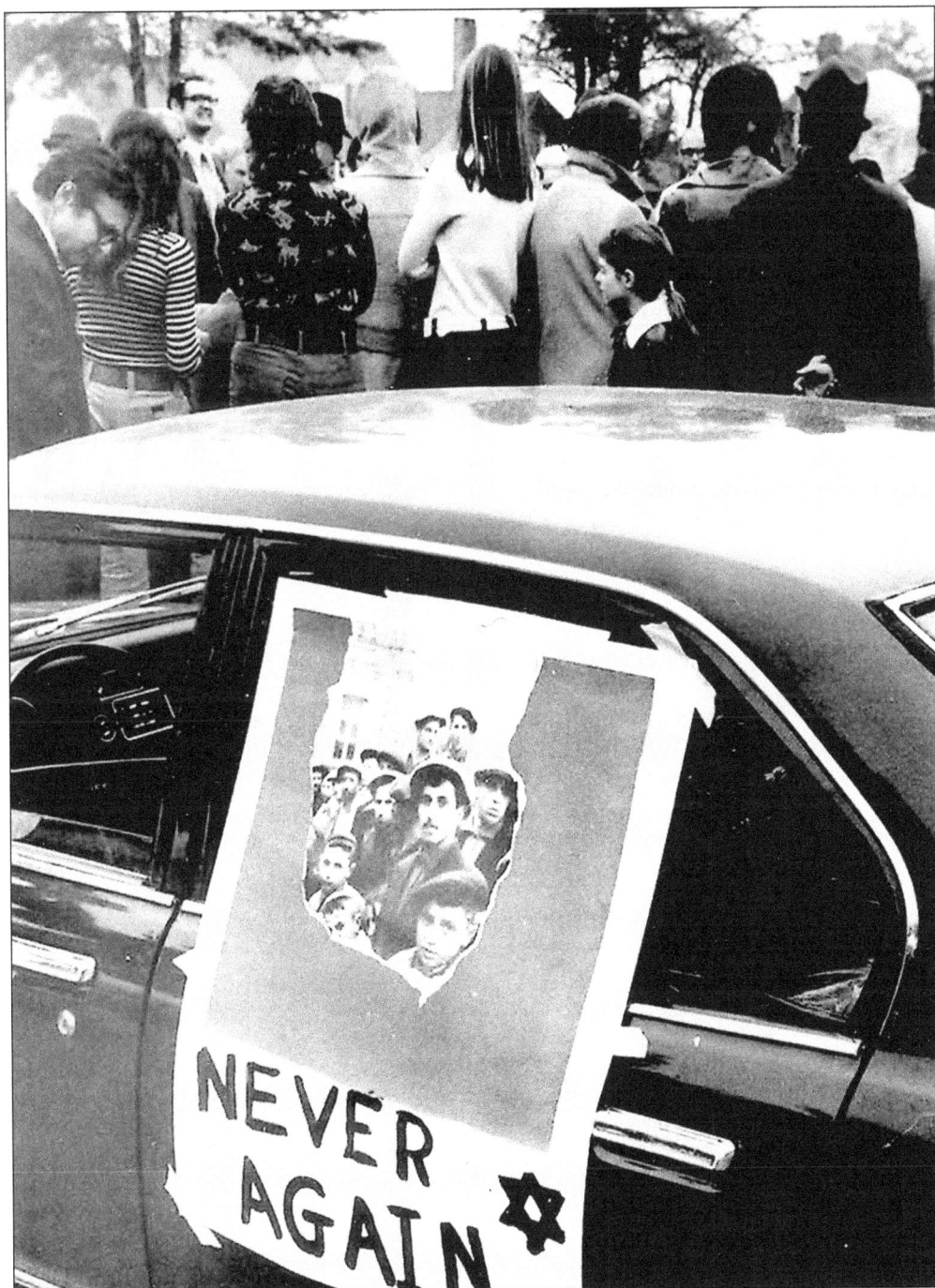

In a demonstration by the Jewish community at Memorial Park in Windsor on October 25, 1971, protestors gathered to speak out against the Soviet Union and Premier Alexei Kosygin's treatment of Jews in Russia. The Never Again poster announces that the Jewish community will remember what happened in the Holocaust during World War II and will remember not to let an event like that happen again. (Courtesy of Rabbi Jonathan V. Plaut; photograph by the Windsor Star.)

The Canadian flag is dipped during a dedication ceremony on October 5, 1970, of a memorial for Jewish soldiers from Windsor who died in World War I and World War II. (Courtesy of Rabbi Jonathan V. Plaut; photograph by the Windsor Star.)

Four

METROPOLITAN
SATELLITES
ANN ARBOR, YPSILANTI, AND FLINT

At the periphery of the Metropolitan Detroit region are the smaller cities of Ann Arbor, Flint, and Ypsilanti. Since 1945, these urban areas have gradually begun to grow together. Ann Arbor is home to the University of Michigan, which has several thousand Jewish students and most of these are from the Jewish community of Metro Detroit. Ypsilanti is home to Eastern Michigan University, which has a couple hundred Jewish students from the Metro Detroit area as well. Due to these circumstances, the Jews living in Ann Arbor and Ypsilanti are intrinsically tied to the heart of the Jewish community that lives in suburban Detroit. Furthermore, thousands of Jewish University of Michigan and Eastern Michigan University alumni live throughout the Detroit suburbs. Flint, in many ways, is also interconnected with the Jewish Metro Detroit community. The University of Michigan Flint campus is located there, which parallels the connections that Ann Arbor and Ypsilanti have. However, Flint's industrial based economy is bounded to the fate of Detroit's industrial economy, and thus has copied its booms and busts. Pictured above is Rabbi Alter Goldstein of the University of Michigan–Ann Arbor Chabad House with fellow students at a Detroit Pistons game in suburban Auburn Hills. (Courtesy of the University of Michigan–Ann Arbor Chabad House.)

Pictured above is Rebbetzin Goldstein, of the Ann Arbor Chabad House, explaining to a student the meaning behind the lulav and etrog during the holiday of Sukkot. Chabad is a philosophy, movement, and organization that assists Jewish people with coming closer to Judaism, and it is run by a group of Chassidim known as Lubaviticher. The Lubaviticher Chassidim originated from the town of Lubavitich in present day Belarus; however, there is a substantially large number that reside within the Jewish community of Metro Detroit. (Courtesy of the University of Michigan–Ann Arbor Chabad House.)

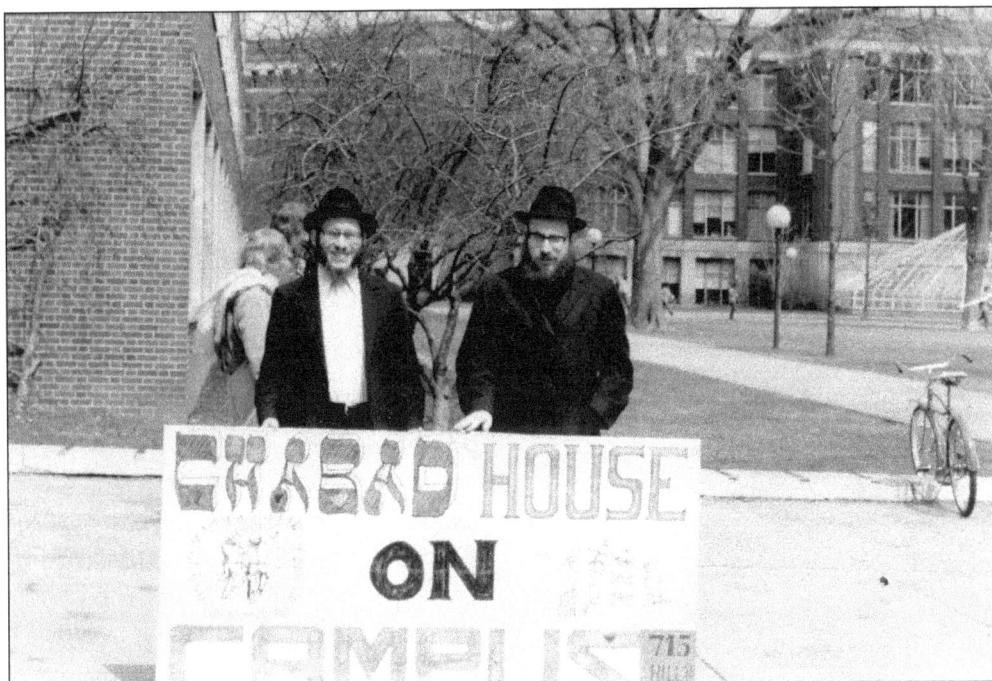

Chabad has been in Ann Arbor on the University of Michigan campus since the late 1970s. Pictured above is Rabbi Aharon Goldstein (right) with his advertising assistant near the Diag on the central campus. (Courtesy of the University of Michigan–Ann Arbor Chabad House.)

A Lubaviticher yeshiva bocher from Oak Park volunteers to help build the sukkah at the Ann Arbor Chabad House in 1999. *Yeshiva bocher* means a student who studies in a Jewish seminary, in Yiddish. Student volunteers often come from Oak Park to give a helping hand in promoting Chabad activities and events at the University of Michigan. (Courtesy of the University of Michigan–Ann Arbor Chabad House.)

A Lubaviticher scribe visiting from Oak Park demonstrates for students at the Diag on the University of Michigan central campus how Hebrew calligraphy is written for sacred texts, such as Torahs, tefillin, and mezuzahs. (Courtesy of the University of Michigan–Ann Arbor Chabad House.)

University of Michigan students glance over a Yiddish newspaper, called *Der Blatt*, and discuss issues pertaining to Orthodox Judaism. (Courtesy of the University of Michigan–Ann Arbor Chabad House.)

Matzo for Passover is made with only two ingredients, extra-fine ground floor and water. The majority of Jews buy their matzo in a grocery store, which usually comes in a square box. Ann Arbor Chabad demonstrates how matzos are made for Passover at a local grocery store in order to show people the process of what goes into making it. The process requires that all matzo be made in less than 18 minutes, from the time the ingredients are mixed to when it comes out of the baking oven. (Courtesy of the University of Michigan–Ann Arbor Chabad House.)

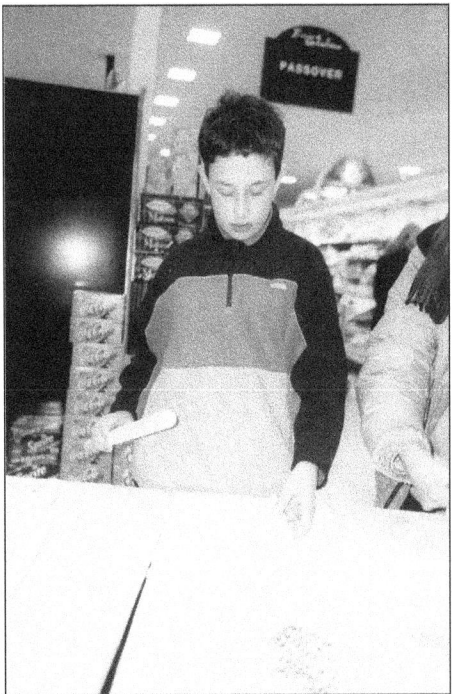

A young baker works making matzos at Ann Arbor Chabad's demonstration at a local grocery store. Traditionally all matzo was made by hand in this fashion, before mechanization. There is, however, a strong demand for authentic handmade matzo, especially the shmurah variety. (Courtesy of the University of Michigan–Ann Arbor Chabad House.)

Since most Metro Detroit Jewish students at the University of Michigan are busy with classes and homework, Ann Arbor Chabad brings the celebration into the campus dormitories so that they do not miss out on the fun of the holiday. Pictured here are students lighting a menorah at Chabad's annual Hanukah party in the dormitories. (Courtesy of the University of Michigan–Ann Arbor Chabad House.)

A Jewish college student wearing his tefillin at the Ann Arbor Chabad House poses for the camera just after praying. Chabad house is also a functioning synagogue in Ann Arbor, and many of its members are Jewish students and alumni from the Jewish community of Metro Detroit. (Courtesy of the University of Michigan–Ann Arbor Chabad House.)

Like a castle on a hill, Ann Arbor Chabad House represents a home away from home for the 6,000 Jewish students that attend the University of Michigan, of which the majority are from the Jewish Community of Metro Detroit. The state office of Chabad-Lubavitch of Michigan is based out of Oak Park. (Courtesy of the University of Michigan–Ann Arbor Chabad House.)

The Jewish Resource Center, known as the JRC, at the University of Michigan was founded in 1999 as a place of learning for college students who want to know more about Judaism, including a successful Maimonides Fellowship program. The Jewish Resource Center and the Maimonides Fellowship were founded by Rabbi Avraham Jacobowitz of Oak Park, who also runs the Machon L'Torah program there. (Courtesy of the private collection of Barry Stiefel.)

The Mandell L. Berman Center for University of Michigan Hillel was built in 1989 by the generous support of Metro Jewish Detroiters. The building is named in honor of Mandell L. Berman, a resident of suburban Detroit who has been a generous patron of University of Michigan Hillel for decades. The Ann Arbor Orthodox Minyan also meets at this building for worship on a daily basis. (Courtesy of the private collection of Barry Stiefel.)

From left to right, Jocelyn Gotlib, Beth Kander, Ilana Goldszer, Jeff Herbstman, Andrea Gilman, and Rena Wexelberg comprised the University of Michigan Hillel 2005 Alternative Winter Break contingent that volunteered to go to Gulfport, Mississippi, to help in the recovery efforts in the aftermath of hurricane Katrina. Congregation Shaarey Zedek of Southfield generously sponsored the students so that the students could volunteer without incurring any expenses on themselves. (Courtesy of the private collection of Barry Stiefel.)

The Ann Arbor Holocaust Memorial stands in a small park next to the Rackham Building on the University of Michigan campus. The bronze sculpture was erected by the generous contributions of many from the Jewish community of Metro Detroit. (Courtesy of the private collection of Barry Stiefel.)

Pictured here is the Eastern Michigan University (EMU) Hillel building in Ypsilanti. Eastern Michigan University Hillel is under the umbrella of the larger Hillel chapter, Hillel of Metro Detroit. (Courtesy of the Eastern Michigan University Hillel.)

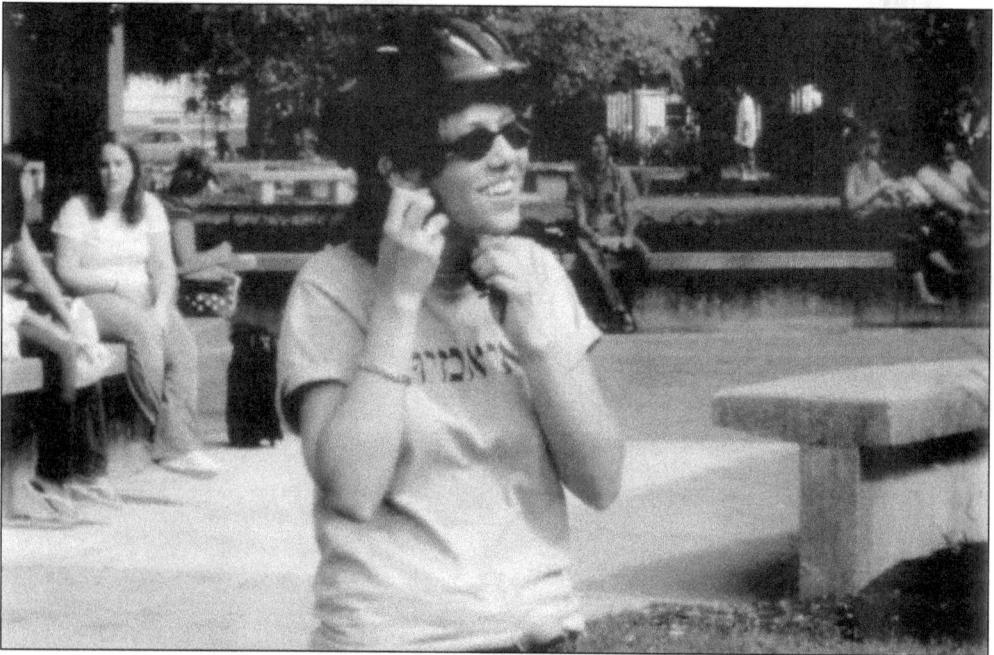

A Jewish Eastern Michigan University student dons her bike helmet, wearing a T-shirt that reads *Ee-m-oo*, or "EMU," in Hebrew. Eastern Michigan University's student body is evenly split between resident on-campus students and commuter off-campus students. Most of these students commute from the Detroit suburbs. (Courtesy of Eastern Michigan University.)

A Jewish Eastern Michigan University student jams on his guitar at Hillel's pre-Passover Bread Fest. There is a tradition of gorging on leavened baked products, such as breads and cakes, just before Passover in order to clean one's pantry for the holiday because leavened baked products are forbidden and why matzo is eaten instead. (Courtesy of the Eastern Michigan University Hillel.)

High rollers have fun and take their chances at an Eastern Michigan University Hillel Hanukah party. Fortunes in chocolate coins and other candies were won and lost while the students took a break from their studies. (Courtesy of Eastern Michigan University.)

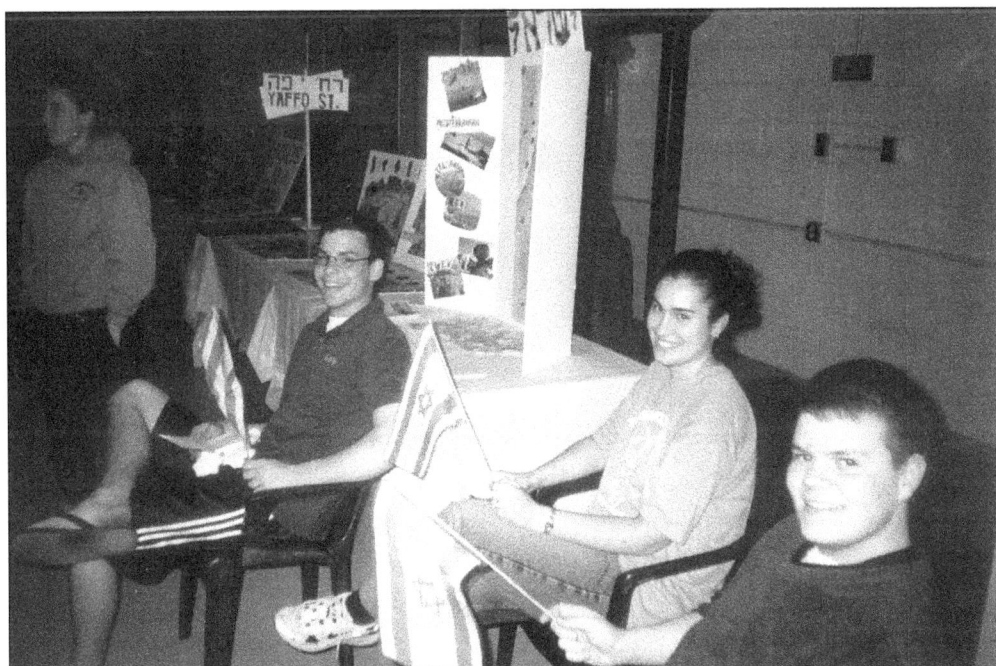

Eastern Michigan University Hillel celebrates Israel's Independence with a rock-climbing event at an indoor gym in Ann Arbor. Since Eastern Michigan University has a significant commuter student demographic, social activities are often planned in and around the campus area to meet the needs of all students. (Courtesy of the Eastern Michigan University Hillel.)

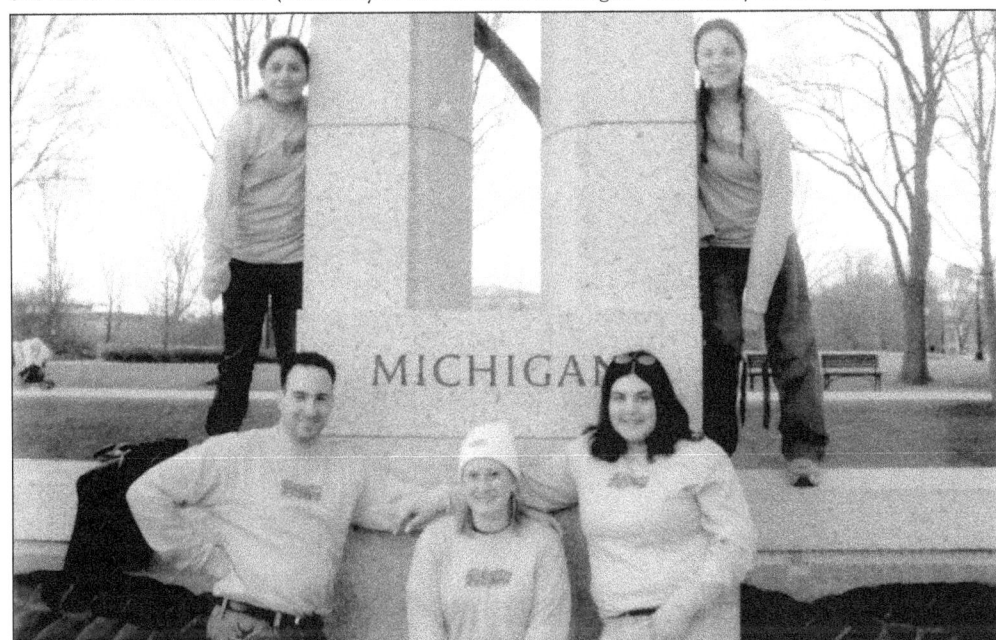

Eastern Michigan University Hillel students pose for a picture on their Alternative Spring Break trip. Alternative Spring Break is a program that college students across the country participate in where they spend their break during the spring semester volunteering on a community service project. (Courtesy of the Eastern Michigan University Hillel.)

Eastern Michigan University Hillel remembers the 1970s with tie-dye T-shirts and challah covers. (Courtesy of the Eastern Michigan University Hillel.)

The Jewish Community Center of Washtenaw County in Ann Arbor is used by a variety of different groups, including the Hebrew Day School. The center often hosts guest speakers and instructors for events from suburban Detroit. (Courtesy of the private collection of Barry Stiefel.)

Pictured here is Congregation Beth Israel, a conservative congregation in Ann Arbor. (Courtesy of the private collection of Barry Stiefel.)

Temple Beth Emeth of Ann Arbor is a reform congregation that shares its building with an Episcopal congregation, called St. Claire of Assisi. The two congregations do not intermix their services, but perform them in the same building at separate times (the Jews on Saturday and the Episcopalians on Sunday). The interior space of the building has been designed by the architect to be interchangeable between the two religions. The two congregations have coexisted in this relationship since the 1970s, and both have planted their respective religious symbols at the front of the building to announce their presence and partnership. (Courtesy of the private collection of Barry Stiefel.)

Beth Israel of Flint hosts a service honoring Flint Jewish Veterans of Foreign Wars, around 1948. Pictured from left to right are B. F. Krasner, Barney Herschon, Sam Sater, and Dr. Robert Rosen of Detroit. The Flint and Detroit Jewish Veterans of Foreign Wars, now known as the Jewish War Veterans of the United States, often had joint functions together. (Courtesy of the Sloan Archives.)

In 1953 there was the United Jewish Appeal of Flint Fundraiser Dinner. The United Jewish Appeal, now known as the United Jewish Communities, does philanthropic work with Jewish and non-Jewish charities throughout the local communities. (Courtesy of the Sloan Archives.)

The Flint Jewish community salutes Israel's 10th anniversary of independence in 1958, which was a cause for celebration throughout Metro Detroit. (Courtesy of the Sloan Archives.)

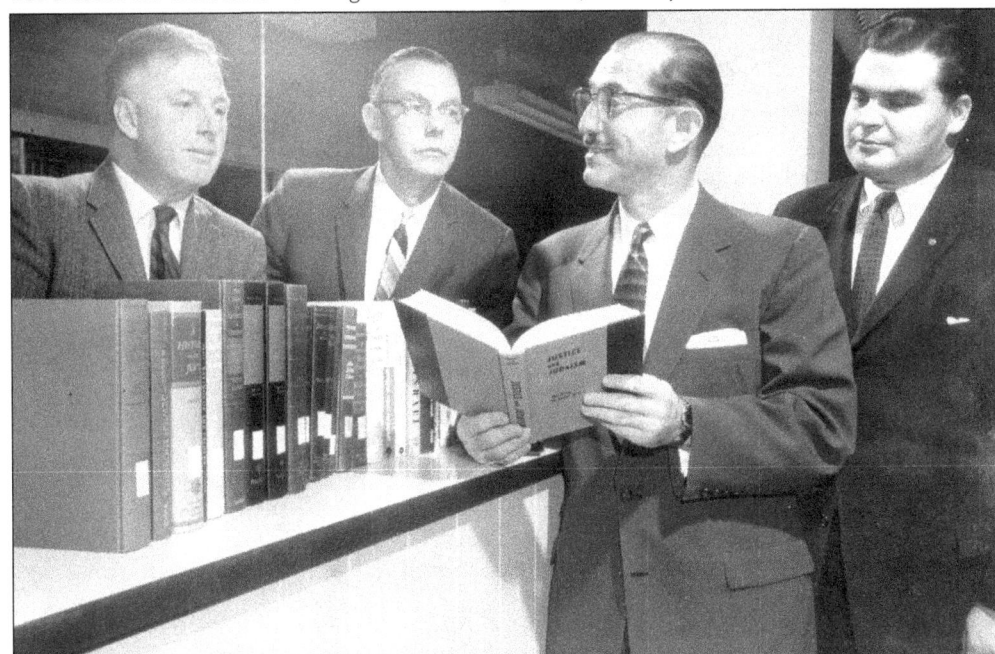

The Flint Jewish community donates important Jewish books to the Flint College Library in 1959 in order to promote education of Jewish history and culture. Flint College was renamed the University of Michigan–Flint in 1971, and many of its students are from Flint and suburban Detroit. (Courtesy of the Sloan Archives.)

Flint B'nai Brith softball team poses for a team photograph during the 1970s. Recreational sports are a popular pastime of Jewish organizations and clubs throughout the Metro Detroit area. (Courtesy of the Sloan Archives.)

Flint's Jewish Girl Scouts give a salute in 1952. Girl Scouting has been just as influential in the childhoods of young women in the Jewish community of Metro Detroit as Boy Scouting has been for young men. (Courtesy of the Sloan Archives.)

Young congregants of Temple Beth El in Flint plant trees at their building in 1950. Planting tress is symbolic of establishing social and communal roots, and because generations of Jews have established their roots in Metro Detroit, the Jewish community is very strong. (Courtesy of the Sloan Archives.)

The Temple Beth El Religious School poses for their annual school picture in 1952. (Courtesy of the Sloan Archives.)

Jewish children from Flint decorate a sukkah in 1951. As the images of this book have demonstrated, participating in Jewish and religious activities have been an important and fun part of making and maintaining a Metro Detroit Jewish community. (Courtesy of the Sloan Archives.)

Jews from all over the United States and Michigan participate in an international solidarity march in Israel during the fall of 1975, just two years after the Yom Kippur War. (Courtesy of

the Sloan Archives.)

Four beautiful Queen Esthers at Beth Israel's Purim party in Flint are pictured in 1947. Throughout Metro Detroit, children dress-up in costumes and have fun during the holiday of Purim. (Courtesy of the Sloan Archives.)

The Jews of Flint and much of the community throughout Metro Detroit organized in 1977 to protest the poor treatment of Russian Jews in the Soviet Union. (Courtesy of the Sloan Archives.)

This is a special dinner hosted by the Institute for American Democracy in Flint promoting racial and religious toleration in the 1950s. Events such as this took place on the eve of the civil rights movement throughout Metro Detroit in order to improve relations between different religious and racial groups. (Courtesy of the Sloan Archives.)

BIBLIOGRAPHY

Bolkosky, Sidney. *Harmony & Dissonance: Voices of Jewish Identity in Detroit, 1914–1967*. Detroit: Wayne State University Press, 1991.

Cantor, Judith Levin. *Jews in Michigan*. East Lansing, MI: Michigan State University Press, 2001.

Cohen, Irwin. *Jewish Detroit*. Charleston, SC: Arcadia Publishing, 2002.

INDEX

Visit us at
arcadiapublishing.com